D1245511

LIVING ON PURPOSE

LIVING ON PURPOSE

STORIES ABOUT FAITH, FORTUNE,
AND FITNESS THAT WILL LEAD YOU
TO AN EXTRAORDINARY LIFE

BRANDON STEINER

LIONCREST
PUBLISHING

LIVING ON PURPOSE

Stories about Faith, Fortune, and Fitness That
Will Lead You to an Extraordinary Life

ISBN   978-1-5445-1288-4 *Hardcover*

       978-1-5445-1287-7 *Paperback*

       978-1-5445-1286-0 *Ebook*

A lot of people ask me about my aha moment when I was on my road to success. To be honest, I don't know the answer to that question. What I do know is the big break, the huge break, the game-changing break came when my wife said yes to marrying me thirty years ago.

Mara, you're the biggest and best break I ever got...period!

CONTENTS

PREFACE

"I'm not complaining, I'm explaining. I'm very grateful and blessed by the life that I've been given."

This book is about faith, fortune, and fitness, but not in the way you might think.

You may have picked up this book expecting to learn the secrets and shortcuts that will help you grow closer to God, become rich, and lose weight without all the hassle and hard work. Here's the real secret: there are no shortcuts to extraordinary achievement in these areas. Our society loves instant results, but anything worth doing can't be achieved overnight. If you really want shortcuts, though, here are a few to consider:

· The fastest way to get closer to God is to die.

- A fast path to riches is to get close with a wealthy uncle and hope they croak, leaving you with a hefty inheritance. Or you could buy lottery tickets and hope you win.
- If you're dying to lose weight overnight, you could cut off an arm or a limb.

You see what I mean? There are no shortcuts with your faith, fortune, and fitness. If you want to achieve extraordinary things, it will require an extraordinary effort and a deeply rooted purpose. Not just any purpose, though. You need the right purpose so you end up where you want to be and not way off course, which is where I found myself in 2002.

ON THE WAY TO RICHES, I BANKRUPTED MYSELF

"You're always on the right path. Sometimes you're just not managing it well and you're taking a detour."

—CAROLINE MYSS

In August of 2000, I sold my company, Steiner Sports, to the Omnicom Group. As part of that process, I accepted a buyout that paid me more money than I ever dreamed I could have. After working nonstop since I was ten, I didn't have to work another day in my life. I should have been on top of the world, as all my hard work had finally paid off in a huge way.

But after putting in relentless effort and long hours to build a company—and frankly, an industry—for close to two decades, I was emotionally bankrupt after selling my company. To sustain that kind of run, I had to go to some deep, dark places emotionally, and those decisions took a toll on me.

I'd been climbing my ladder to success and reached the top after many years, only to look down and realize the ground underneath my ladder was unstable and possibly leaning against the wrong building.

I lost friendships because I wasn't a good friend. Friends would call me to get together, and I could barely hold a two-minute conversation. My mental response when asked for a good time to get together with someone was often, *How about never?*

I wasn't the husband or father I wanted to be during that time either. A lot of people, myself included, mistakenly think that because we provide a comfortable living for our families—nice house, cars, vacations—the relationships at home are healthy. Providing for your family is important, but it doesn't trump being there for your spouse and your kids. You don't win Parent of the Year simply because you bring home a big paycheck.

My health also suffered. Not only was I highly stressed,

but I'd eaten poorly and let my weight get away from me. On top of that, I'd developed kidney stones, which I'm pretty sure was related to my high stress levels and my poor diet.

I was at a critical juncture in my life. I could continue to focus primarily on making more money, or I could seek new, more meaningful purposes. I'm not ashamed to admit I struggled with this decision. The mindset I'd had since I was a kid hustling on the streets of my neighborhood was that I had to work hard to survive. My highway didn't have a lot of lanes, and I'd gotten pretty comfortable in the fast one. It was hard for me to grasp the importance of anything other than grinding it out to make my business more successful (making even more money).

It took me several years, but with some help from people I trust, I discovered several new purposes that have fueled my life since selling my company:

- I wanted to be a better husband and father by being more sensitive to what was going on in the lives of my wife and kids.
- I wanted my company, Steiner Sports, to use our success for something other than making more money. We'd done some charity work, but I wanted to bring those efforts to the forefront so we could give back and help people even more.

- I wanted to leave a legacy that was worth remembering. As I grappled with the idea of significance versus success, I had to ask myself if I wanted to die having made a lot of money or having made an impact on people. I chose to make an impact.

Everything extraordinary that's happened in my life started with a purpose. If you think your purpose has to be grand, elaborate, or selfless, you're wrong. A purpose can be anything that motivates you to work hard, think more, or feel inspired.

INTRODUCTION

"If you have a life, you have a purpose."

—CAROLINE MYSS

After selling my company, I set out on a mission to change my life. I wanted to add more meaning to all areas of my life and become well rounded. To do that, I knew I needed to find some gurus who could help me improve my physical health, mental health, and relationships. But first, I needed to change the most important thing: my perspective.

If you're stuck in how you view things, you'll be stuck in how you do things. To show you what I mean, I want to tell you about an overworked, overscheduled businesswoman who was on a typical business trip that wasn't going particularly well.

A businesswoman from Brooklyn was nearing the end of a business trip on the West Coast. She'd spent the past week running from one meeting to the next, so by the time Friday rolled around, she was totally fried. All she could think about was wrapping up her last two appointments and catching her flight back home so she could see her husband and two kids. As she sipped her second coffee of the morning, thoughts of their smiling faces pushed her forward despite the fatigue she felt.

Four hours later, the businesswoman scrambled into a taxi and told the driver to floor it to the airport. Her last meeting had run long, and she was now in danger of missing her flight. If that wasn't enough stress, her anxiety was ramping up as the flight drew closer because she hated flying. She did it just for work and flew only when driving wasn't an option.

As the taxi screeched to a halt at her terminal, she looked at her watch. Thirty minutes until takeoff. She'd hoped to eat lunch after her last meeting, but now she'd have to choose between eating on the flight and grabbing something on her dash through the airport. Stomach rumbling, she snatched her suitcase, paid the driver, and began to sprint.

Once through security, she zoomed into a small shop that was on the way to her gate and grabbed a bag of cookies.

This will have to do, she told herself. She stuffed the bag of cookies in her purse and practically threw the money at the cashier as she resumed her race to the gate. She didn't dare glance at her watch. Her anxiety was high enough already; she didn't need a reminder of how close she was cutting it.

As she rounded the corner and her gate came into view, she saw the gate manager going to shut the door to the jet bridge. The businesswoman threw up her hands and breathlessly yelled, "Wait, I'm coming!"

The gate manager stopped in her tracks, turned around, and smiled as she saw the businesswoman approaching. She opened the door, scanned her boarding pass, and wished her a good flight. Panting, the businesswoman wound her way down the jet bridge, boarded the plane, and squeezed between the rows toward her seat. She was sitting in the back, and as she approached her row, her stomach dropped. Her seat was crammed between two gigantic guys who eyed her with annoyance when they saw she'd be joining them.

What else could go wrong today? she thought. *I'm totally exhausted, I just want to get home, and now I've got to endure a six-hour flight stuffed between these two galoots!*

She crammed her carry-on into the overhead compartment, flopped down in her seat, and closed her eyes. She exhaled and tried to think positively. She'd somehow made her flight, and thanks to the bag of cookies sitting on her tray table, she wouldn't be forced to eat airplane food. She smiled as she reached into the bag and pulled out a cookie.

That smile disappeared when the guy sitting next to the window reached into her bag and took out a cookie of his own. For a moment, the businesswoman was dumb-founded. She chewed her cookie and stared straight ahead, wondering if what she'd just seen had actually happened.

She reached in and grabbed another cookie. The guy next to her did the same thing.

What the hell is wrong with this guy? she fumed. *You can't take someone else's cookies!*

She wanted to say something to the guy, but she was so heated she might start a confrontation that would get her kicked off the plane. Even if she didn't blow her lid, she didn't want to piss off the guy who was already occupying most of her seat space with his massive girth. *Better to sit and stew,* she thought.

This process repeated itself for another ten minutes as the

plane prepared for takeoff. The businesswoman grabbed a cookie, only to have her humongous neighbor grab one too. Once half the bag was gone, she was so incensed that she got up from her seat and walked down the aisle, taking deep breaths and counting to ten. She was ready to rip that jerk's head off for taking her cookies without even asking. She returned to her seat hopeful that he was done pilfering her snacks, but once she took another cookie, that hope disappeared.

Finally, with one cookie left, the guy turned to her and spoke. "You want to split it?" he asked.

The businesswoman waved him off, so enraged by his audacity that her appetite had vanished. After the guy ate the last cookie, she crumpled up the bag and threw it on the floor. *I'm done with this flight*, she thought. She slipped a sleep mask over her eyes and drifted off. Once she awoke, she could get off this plane and away from this cookie-stealing jerk.

When the plane landed, the businesswoman wormed her way to the front of the queue and exited the airplane in a huff. She stormed through the airport, suitcase bouncing along behind her as she walked. Once in the parking garage, she reached into her purse for her car keys.

She gasped.

There in her purse was the bag of cookies she'd bought at the airport.

The businesswoman's perspective during that flight created a story in her head that simply wasn't true. When she found the cookies she'd bought, she realized she'd been looking at her situation all wrong. Have you ever had a moment like the businesswoman when you realized after the fact that your vantage point had kept you from seeing the truth of a situation?

I've been there, and I'm sure you have as well. We're all guilty of being more concerned with who's eating our cookies than with sharing our cookies with others.

To borrow a saying from my daughter, Nicole, "If you smell shit everywhere you walk, you might want to check your shoes."

The way we move through life truly comes down to our perspective. I knew my job going forward was to change my perspective in many areas. I had to approach my life the same way I approached making money. **I needed to start living my life for a living.**

If you want to be extraordinary in all areas of your life, including family, fitness, faith, and fortune, it starts with purpose and the right perspective.

I cringe when I read a book or hear a speaker claiming this process begins with passion. You hear it all the time: "You gotta have passion!" "Find your passion!"

I was stuck on that idea for a long time, and all it got me was frustration. I eventually realized that I was chasing the wrong thing. Passion is hard to find because it's not the natural starting point of your journey to extraordinary achievement. If you're looking for a train, you're better off looking for a train station. If you need food, go to the supermarket.

If you want to find your passion, start with a purpose. Passion is not the initiator. It is the by-product of finding your purpose and then being committed to pursuing it.

Remember this formula: *Purpose + Commitment = Passion.*

I started to think about my journey to extraordinary achievement like a tree. The roots are my purpose, in that they help me stay anchored. Commitment is the trunk of the tree, growing little by little every day as it stretches skyward toward the sun. The branches that grow off that trunk represent my passion, and the fruit or leaves are traits like creativity, clarity, focus, determination, diligence, and thoughtfulness that are ignited by my passion. (Note to the young ones who are reading this: sorry, there are no apps or shortcuts for these extraordinary traits. You've got to earn them.)

I had been chasing passion and, to some degree, coming up empty. Now I knew I'd been chasing the wrong thing. I had to begin pursuing purpose and passion would follow.

DO I HAVE A WINNABLE GAME?

When I set out to redefine my purpose, I asked myself if I had a winnable game and if the people around me could help me win. The answer to those questions was no. I didn't have the right diet, and I wasn't getting the proper amount of quality sleep. I didn't have the right people around to help me get where I wanted to go.

As a result, I had to redefine what winning looked like for me and the most important people around me. Doing this allowed me to create new goals I could pursue.

A goal is important because it gives me something to shoot for, but a goal by itself is not enough. I need to dig deep to discover why I want to accomplish this goal.

When I think about winning, I need a collective group of *whys* to surround my goal.

If you want to lose weight, ask yourself *why* before you start dieting and exercising. I had a closet full of clothes I couldn't fit into. I also hadn't played basketball in three years. My *whys* were to be able to play my favorite sport again and fit into all these clothes I'd bought. I'm not going to get into the dollars spent on the clothes I'd purchased over the past years, thinking I'd fit into them once I lost a little weight, but we're talking about ten pairs of jeans, six suits, eight pairs of dress slacks, and that's just part of it.

You need the roots of purpose to take hold so that you

aren't easily knocked off track. You'll also find that your thought process begins to change when you live with purpose. A newfound sense of optimism begins to grow inside you, leading to greater self-confidence. Your days will be fuller and more meaningful when you approach them with this mindset.

With these factors working in your favor, you'll feel an undeniable momentum propelling you forward. You'll become like a locomotive—highly motivated and hard to stop.

Purpose is too important to be deferred. I decided I deserved better than shuffling through a passionless life, working to make money so I could afford things I didn't need in order to impress people I didn't like.

PART I

———

FAITH

CHAPTER 1

FAITH OR FEAR

"If faith doesn't fit through the door that opens, don't go through it."

I met Mariano Rivera, the legendary closer for the New York Yankees, in 1998. A company called us about getting autographed baseballs before the World Series, which featured the Yankees and the San Diego Padres. As I went through the Rolodex of Yankee players, they all told us no, because signing baseballs before the World Series was taboo.

We reached the "R" section and called Mariano. He agreed to sign some balls, either because he didn't know better, or he felt sorry for us. So I went to his humble one-bedroom walk-up in New Rochelle to meet him. We sat down and made small talk for a few moments before he stopped signing, looked up, and asked me, "Brandon, do you believe in God?"

The question caught me off guard, but I answered, "Yeah, I believe in God."

He didn't miss a beat. "Do you believe in Jesus Christ?" he asked next.

I looked at him for a second before answering, "Can I get back to you on that?"

The truth is I never understood faith until I met Mariano. I believed in God, but it didn't extend much beyond that. I liked to joke that I prayed almost every day in the 1990s, but it was for the Yankees to win or for Derek Jeter not to get hurt.

Mariano and I have worked together for more than twenty years, and we've had these long conversations while I drove him to various appearances. Inevitably, those talks would turn to subjects of faith. I learned about the specifics of Christianity and how it differed from Judaism. We talked about divine intervention and ways to become a more faithful person, and I have to say, Mariano convinced me with his arguments.

Our relationship started me on a journey of faith that I'm still on to this day. I never thought a skinny kid from

Panama with broken English was going to have such a profound impact on me, but I've come to believe that God gives us signs and uses people to redirect our path sometimes. Whether we choose to acknowledge those signs is up to us.

Mariano's faith was tested in a big way on May 3, 2012, when he tore his ACL catching fly balls in the outfield during batting practice. I was in the kitchen that day helping my wife, Mara, set the table for dinner when I saw the news that Mariano had gotten hurt.

I turned to Mara and said, "Our summer just changed dramatically."

"What do you mean?" she asked.

"We've never had a summer off with Mariano," I told her. "He always tells us no during the summer because he's focused on his family, his faith, and helping the Yankees win. Now that he's injured, he's going to be bored and looking for things to do."

It was true—Mariano had always turned down opportunities to make money during the season because he was solely focused on his job. The remaining time he had was devoted to his wife, his kids, and growing his faith. Our joke was, "What rhymes with Mo? No."

At the same time, I also wondered what was next for my friend. Before the 2012 season, we'd talked quite a bit about retirement. Mariano wasn't sure how long he wanted to keep playing. His His body was worn down, and he was excited about the next phase of his life.

A month after his injury, Mariano called me at the office in a panic, asking me to come over to his house immediately. I asked what was wrong, and he said we'd discuss it when I got there. When I got to the house, Mariano pulled me aside and revealed to me that he was upset. After signing some items I'd brought him to sign, we went inside. When we sat down to talk, he still looked upset, so I asked him what was wrong.

"I need surgery for my ACL," he revealed. "I won't be able to play the rest of this season."

"With a torn ACL, did you really think you were coming back this season?" I asked.

"Yes," he said. "I've been working hard since the injury. Watch this."

Mariano stood up and showed me how he could push off with his injured knee. In my head, I was having a Jerry Seinfeld moment, thinking, *Is this guy crazy? He has a torn ACL!*

Finally, I got Mariano to admit he couldn't move side to side and that surgery was the best route for him to take. He wasn't taking the news well, though. For a guy who was so cool, calm, and collected on the mound, he was having a moment in his house that day.

In that moment, Mariano faced the choice we all face: faith or fear? Fear was pulling at him, tearing down the faith in his doctors and in himself to get healthy and come back next season to end his career on his terms. It was hard for me to see because Mariano is one of the most faith-filled people I've ever met. I chose to remind him of that.

"You have been wondering about what the end of your career would be like," I said. "You wanted to get the church built and to spend more time with your family. God has granted your wish and given you exactly that. He's given you a window into what life will be like after baseball, and you still have the option to come back next year if you want."

Time away from the game was good for Mariano. It allowed him to test-drive his new life and filled him with faith that things would work out in the end. His injury was a temporary setback on the way to a major comeback. Mariano returned to the game recharged, with a new perspective, and without the mystery of what awaits him after baseball. He ended his career the following year on his terms, finishing with forty-four saves and a 2.11 ERA.

Mariano was fueled by purpose after his injury. He wanted to finish his career his way. Remaining in a fearful state could've robbed him of that chance. True to the Mariano I know, he chose to walk by faith, and it made all the difference for him, his family, Yankee fans, his teammates, and everybody who loved watching him play the game.

YOU CAN'T PLAY SCARED

"The cave you fear to enter holds the treasure that you seek."

—JOSEPH CAMPBELL

When people achieve a high level of success, the tendency is to get nervous about what others think or how that level of success will be maintained. As a result of how worried they feel, they'll often stop doing what brought them success in the first place.

I experienced this myself as Steiner Sports began gaining notoriety and more attention came my way. I didn't have experience with our new level of success or making as much money as we were. Honestly, the pressure stifled me a bit. Even living in my new house, I was struggling to get comfortable there. It was only the second house I'd ever lived in.

If athletes tense up in big games, coaches will often tell them to play like they did when they were a kid. There's wisdom in that old coaching cliché. To handle my company's new success, I needed to approach life like I did when I was kid—fearless and filled with faith.

In other words, I had to stop playing scared.

It reminds me of the time I went to watch the Syracuse men's basketball team play Duke and sat right behind the Syracuse bench. The game was at Cameron Indoor Stadium, which is Duke's home court. It's a rowdy, rough place to play. It's extremely intimidating. The fans are right on top of you. There are more Final Four banners and retired numbers than there are people in the arena. It's a legendary building, built in 1940, and holds about 9,000 screaming, crazy fans. There are plenty of reasons to be fearful when you walk into this stadium to play against Coach Krzyzewski and the Duke Blue Devils.

My beloved Orange had a terrible first half. The players were tight, and the score was ugly at halftime. Syracuse managed just sixteen points. About ten minutes into the game, Syracuse Coach Jim Boeheim called a timeout and huddled with his players on the bench. I leaned in close to hear how Coach would snap his players out of their funk.

"You cannot play this game scared," he told the team. He

repeated the line twice more for emphasis. The players were locked into what he was saying. As Coach spoke, they all looked at each other, nodding their heads in agreement. They knew that if they didn't shake off the fear they felt right now, the game would be over. Duke would pummel them.

I sat back in my seat, curious to see how the Syracuse players would respond. I was happy to see them loosen up throughout the rest of the first half and perform better in the second half. They couldn't overcome the hole they dug for themselves and ended up losing the game, but the advice Boeheim gave his players during that timeout stuck with me. After a sluggish start, Coach knew the culprit wasn't poor mechanics or a lack of effort. His guys were playing scared. It showed when they passed up open jumpers, refused to attack the basket, didn't crash the boards, and committed careless turnovers.

Once they stepped out of that fear and into faith—in the game plan, their coach, and each other—they started playing up to their potential and gave Duke all they could handle.

My question to you is: Are you playing scared right now?

I was seeing a lot of people around me at different stages of life who played scared. The thought of switching jobs or asking for a raise, or growing closer with their spouse and children, terrifies them. They're scared of failure, but they're also scared of success. I've often seen people with the means to do something different with their lives who would rather play not to lose instead of play to win. I have to include myself in that group.

The past few years, I've been focused on getting out of that fearful state and into a faithful one. I've always been confident in my ability to make money. What I wanted was to have that same confidence when it came to being faithful, growing closer with my family, being a better friend, and being a more kind and generous person.

A fine line exists between fear and faith, so you have to be mindful of which side you're on in any given situation. The side of fear is a steep, slippery slope. When you slide into fear, you'll find it's easy to keep sliding and difficult to climb out. The good news is that faith works the same way, but in the opposite direction. Like a train rolling downhill, once you start living faithfully, you'll approach every situation with optimism and joy.

I believe that kind of faithful living is an express road to extraordinary. You're still going to hit some bumps, but those bumps won't leave you on the side of the road. Of course, for this express road to be a viable option, we need to understand what faith means and what extraordinary achievement looks like.

WHAT IS FAITH?

"Faith sees the invisible, believes the unbelievable, and receives the impossible."

—CORRIE TEN BOOM

One of the things Mariano taught me along the way is, "Faith is something you have and you believe in, but you can't see it."

Even though we can't see it, faith can give us strength in every area of our lives.

You can have faith in God or some other higher power to watch over you, guide you, and keep you safe. I've certainly come to believe in divine intervention. There are moments in my life that seemed coincidental at the time, but as I look back at the path I took to get where I am now, it's hard not to believe there was some kind of plan in place.

I always wondered why I was short on faith. As I examined my story more and more, I saw where it broke down at different points along the way. My dad died when I was twelve years old, and I grew up in a broken home where I had to worry about food, clothing, and paying the bills at a very young age. When you look at a situation like that as a kid, you begin to wonder how you can have faith that good things will happen. You wonder if the same thing is going to happen to you when you get older.

Did something happen in your life that fractured your confidence in yourself, in others, or in a higher power? We'll see in a moment the power of disappointment and how negative experiences can supersede all the wonderful things that happen to us. Did you suffer disappointment along the way that changed the story you tell yourself?

When I lack confidence in certain areas of my life, my faith suffers. I have to ask myself what needs to be done to improve my self-confidence and increase my capacity for faith.

I can remove fear from the equation and replace it with faith, but that kind of transformation takes a strategy and consistent execution. It's easier for me to walk in faith when I keep my priorities in check. I spent about 95 percent of my first forty years focused on how to make money and how to make more money, and now I know to focus a lot more time and effort on learning how to improve the other pillars of my life.

Understanding my strategy and having faith in my ability brings me confidence. I'm striving for extraordinary achievement, which always starts with faith. I've used the word *extraordinary* quite a few times in this book without attaching meaning to it. Let's do that now.

SUCCESS VS. SIGNIFICANCE

There is a difference between being great and being extraordinary. Someone who's great works hard, has passion and purpose, and is extremely focused and grateful.

Someone who's extraordinary does all those things and realizes it's not enough. Extraordinary people are always striving to do better, achieve more, and push further.

All throughout my life, I've been driven to be extraordinary. Truthfully, it made me feel odd. I wondered if I was too driven or too greedy. Did I want too much? Were my expectations unrealistic? I struggled with those feelings for a long time.

That changed when I met Brendon Burchard, author of several best-selling books, many of which focus on faith. We met in Arizona at a Harvey Mackay Roundtable, and I convinced him to meet up with me for dinner and a Bruce Springsteen concert back in New York.

In talking with Brendon and reading his book *High Per-*

formance Habits, I realized the extraordinary traits that I wrestled with were typical of high-performance individuals, some of whom Brendon interviewed in his book. As I read their stories, I felt a sense of relief. Brendon's book helped me see that extraordinary people don't settle for greatness because they know there's something even greater out there waiting for them—significance.

This was the first time I didn't feel odd for scheming and dreaming or for thinking about what else or what's next. This book helped me feel normal.

I also learned about the qualities extraordinary people possess. Brendon says extraordinary people aren't afraid to ask for help. They understand that achieving extraordinary success often means collaborating with other talented, committed people. This sense of inclusion extends to their families, where everyone's input is valued.

Extraordinary people are also unafraid to make a mess, since they usually start with a concept that's never been tested. Thomas Edison didn't set out to invent a better candle. Henry Ford didn't want to make a faster horse and buggy.

Extraordinary people don't stop when chaos reigns. They push through to bring order to the mess they've made. These are people who know the value of unraveling something to make it better than before and relish that challenge.

You should set the bar for extraordinary achievement high and create a finish line in many areas of your life. Extraordinary people are always measuring. Most people don't want to deal with the real results. If you're measuring what you have, you're living in reality. Crossing that finish line is part of what makes it extraordinary. The other part—the more worthwhile part, in my opinion—is how you get there.

Faith will start you on the express road to extraordinary, but there will still be bumps along the way. When unexpected hardships pop up, you're confronted with the same choice you've had all along: walk by faith through the storm or retreat in fear.

HOW WNBA STAR BRITTNEY SYKES DEFEATED FEAR

"Let your hopes, not your hurts, shape your future."

—ROBERT H. SCHULLER

Brittney Sykes knows all too well how fear can threaten your faith when hardships strike. Brittney is from Newark, New Jersey, and played college basketball at Syracuse.

She was drafted at number seven overall in the 2017 WNBA draft, the highest selected women's basketball player in school history. Brittney was a McDonald's All-American in high school and was the highest rated recruit Syracuse had ever landed up to that point. The team saw immediate success with her in the lineup, winning its first NCAA tournament game against Chattanooga in 2014, which was her sophomore season.

That was also the game in which Brittney tore the ACL in her right knee.

Ten months of rehab followed her injury. If you know anything about coming back from an ACL tear, it's physically and mentally grueling. Fear can swallow you up pretty fast as months go by without stepping foot on the court. Nevertheless, Brittney persisted in faith and worked her way back. She managed to return to action a few games before the team's showdown with number-four-ranked Notre Dame. The jubilation felt by those who supported Brittney through her rehab turned to heartbreak when she went down with a knee injury in the first half. Her worst nightmare was confirmed shortly after the game ended—a torn right ACL, the same one she'd just spent ten months rehabbing.

Can you imagine how it must've felt to receive that news? I'd have been gutted.

At this point, Brittney easily could've listened to the voice in her head saying, *Maybe this isn't for me*. Nobody would've blamed her for walking away after tearing her ACL for the second time in ten months. But that wasn't Brittney.

I'd been spending time with Brittney and her teammates for a couple years leading up to the 2015 season. I'd been working with Quentin Hillsman, the head women's basketball coach at Syracuse, to develop a strategy for the upcoming season. Quentin has been the head women's basketball coach since 2006 and has helped turn that program into a national powerhouse among the likes of UConn and Tennessee.

With help from the players, we wanted to define what it meant to play for Syracuse women's basketball. What kind of legacy did this team want to leave?

During my first talk with the players, I told them I'd bought plane tickets for Indianapolis, home of the Final Four that year, and I expected to see them there. In my mind, anything less than a Final Four appearance would be a disappointment, given the talent level on that team. I knew, however, that getting Brittney involved would be crucial to Syracuse making a deep run. Brianna Butler and Alexis Peterson could carry the team offensively, but come tournament time, they would need Brittney to step up her offensive output.

As the NCAA tournament drew near in February, Syracuse had lost some games but was playing well overall. Brittney, I noticed, had moments when she looked hesitant. You could tell she was playing scared. Again, I didn't blame her after two ACL tears and months of rehab, but if Syracuse wanted to make a Final Four run, they needed the preinjury version of Brittney who slashed through the lane and crashed the glass with no fear.

After the game against Georgia Tech, I asked Brittney how she felt.

"I feel fine," she replied. "I'm like 99 percent there."

"The difference between 99 percent and 100 percent is 100 percent," I told her. "The reason I ask is because you look hesitant about going hard to the basket, like maybe you're afraid to hurt your knee again. You seem to be a little nervous."

"Oh," she said, looking reflective. "I hadn't really thought about that."

"Look, you're one of the best players on this team, if not one of the best players in this league," I told her. "I think it's time to reintroduce yourself to your teammates and coaches, but before you can do that, I think you need to reintroduce yourself to yourself. Teams need to be afraid whenever you've got the ball, but right now, they're not. You have to believe in yourself and have faith, not fear, in your game. When you do, teams won't be able to stop you at all."

I was working to convert her fear into faith. To drive the point home, I left her with a half-joking threat, "If you don't put up fifteen a night the rest of the way, I'll be back!"

Four nights later against Virginia, Brittney scored seventeen points. She averaged thirteen points per game the rest of the season, and Syracuse exceeded its goal of making a Final Four, losing to an undefeated UConn team in the national championship game.

Brittney had all the physical tools to help lead her team to a title game. She simply had to decide that fear wasn't going to dictate how she played on the court. Syracuse was a team with a purpose that year, and Brittney carried her own purpose—to show people back in Newark that she was the real deal and to make good for her mom, who'd always supported her. When Brittney combined those twin purposes with a renewed faith in her game, Syracuse became the force of nature it was destined to be and accomplished things no other team in school history had done. She carried that success into her first year with the Atlanta Dream, averaging 13.9 points per game and receiving votes for Rookie of the Year.

From two ACL tears to a top rookie in the WNBA—that's the power of faith.

"Challenges are what make life interesting. Overcoming them is what makes life meaningful."

—JOSHUA J. MARINE

TWO IMPORTANT ASPECTS OF PURPOSE

"You should never view your challenges as a disadvantage. Instead, it's important for you to understand that your experience facing and overcoming adversity is actually one of your biggest advantages."

—MICHELLE OBAMA

Brittney and her teammates were propelled by a purpose: make it to the Final Four. I think this example illustrates two important points about finding your own purpose.

The first is that winning isn't always self-centered. Sometimes it is. My friend Dan Clark, who was a contributor to the *Chicken Soup for the Soul* series, likes to say, "There's no 'I' in team, but there are two 'i's' in winning." Brittney needed to be selfish with her scoring to help her team win, but in a larger sense, she alone didn't define what winning meant for the Syracuse women's basketball team. It was the entire squad working together to identify a purpose that could unify and motivate them during a long and challenging season. At that time, I realized winning was a lot more than just the score.

When you make purpose all about you, it can set you down a path that diverges from your spouse, your kids, or your boss. Even if you achieve something extraordinary, is it worth celebrating if you've isolated everyone important in your life?

The second lesson from Brittney's story is you have to execute your purpose. As my friend Joe Plumeri, author of *The Power of Being Yourself* and vice chairman of the First Data board of directors, likes to say, "Execution eats strategy for lunch." Brittney and her teammates knew that words wouldn't be enough to get them to the Final Four. They needed a strategy that would put them over the top.

We bounced around ideas of what that strategy would be before settling on this mantra for the season: "We will be the most relentless defensive team in the country. We will take everything away from you, even your next breath."

I loved that strategy, but I knew it would require unbelievable conditioning to execute. When I asked the players to rank their conditioning on a scale of one to ten, most of them sheepishly admitted they were at a seven. They knew they needed to exercise with more intensity, control everything they ate, and get enough sleep every night.

To their credit, they did everything required to be the most relentless defensive team in the country, and that effort paid off with the school's first trip to the Final Four.

Most people can identify what winning means to them, but few are willing to do the things needed to achieve that purpose. Tying back into our first point, what helps the most when you're starting down this path is to ask for help. Pull people into your journey who are seeking the same extraordinary achievement so you can encourage and support one another. Finding a shared purpose with family members, teammates, or coworkers isn't just the selfless thing to do. It's the smart thing to do. Everyone finds strength when they've got people they care about pulling in the same direction as them.

YOU NEED MORE THAN ONE *WHY*

After this lesson, I looked at what winning meant to me, and I realized I needed to come up with a new set of *whys* and bring some of my old *whys* into focus. Why did I start in the sports business? Why did I want to own my own company? Why did I want to get married? Why did I want to have a family? Why did I want to have the best health possible?

Purpose comes from answering that question: Why do I want to do this? One *why* can carry you in the short term, but the key to achieving a purpose that is long-lasting is finding as many *whys* as you can. The more, the better.

As your life evolves and changes, the *why* you defined a decade ago may no longer fit your life now or motivate you like it once did. With something like marriage, it's crucial to have not just one *why*, but a bucketful of them. I had several *whys* when I married my wife:

- She's the most beautiful woman I've ever seen.
- She's got that spunk and personality that I love.
- I knew she'd be the best mother to our kids one day.
- She always tells me the truth, whether I want to hear it or not!
- She's a great partner in every area of my life.
- The way she rolls her eyes when I tell her about a new scheme for the day.

"A great marriage is not when the 'perfect couple' comes together. It is when an imperfect couple learns to enjoy their differences."

—DAVE MEURER

Throughout the course of our marriage, each of these reasons has motivated me to resolve an argument, reach a compromise, or look for ways I can serve her. My big bucketful of *whys* is one of the main reasons we've had a successful marriage for thirty years.

I wanted my purpose with fitness to be a healthy, functioning body. Winning for me was to get my body fat lower so I could have better mobility. In other instances, you might want to improve your health now to fit into your wedding dress. But what happens when that wedding is over and that *why* expires? Do you have others in your bucket to pull out and continue achieving that purpose? Perhaps you want a healthy, functioning body in the future so you can spend time with your grandkids and attend their weddings one day.

Multiple *whys* pull me through when I'm facing adversity. If you go to work for a company solely because you like the boss, imagine how you'd feel if one day you got into a fight with your boss that left you wanting to quit. If your bucket is empty when you reach in there, you might just make a dumb decision based on one argument. But if you also chose that company because it has good benefits, the job is fun, you have a short commute to the office, and there's a possibility for raises and promotions, you won't overreact when a fight with your boss temporarily fries one of your *whys*.

When I hit forty (i.e., halftime), I went into the locker room and examined my game plan. Similar to a sports team, we need to see if we're executing the strategies we've got in place, tweak some things, and come up with some new strategies for the second half of our "game."

I treated my life like a basketball game. In my mid-forties, I called a timeout and took a look at how things were working in my marriage, at work, and with friendships. I saw what I liked and didn't like, then decided to do more of what I liked and less of what I didn't like. I benched a few people and realized a few of the plays I'd called didn't work. Like any good coach, I made adjustments during the game instead of waiting until the end—working out more, cutting down on travel, going to sleep earlier, and seeing friends and family more.

Sometimes you need to invent some new *whys* as the old ones have likely worn out. You can't always anticipate what life will look like two decades after you first discover your purpose. Once you've done a job for fifteen years, the reasons you initially chose that job may have lost their "oomph" years ago. When you've been married for twenty-five years and your kids have left the house, call a timeout with your spouse and create new *whys* that support your definition of winning.

I'm not advocating for the midlife crisis here. What you need to create new *whys* is often right in front of you. One of my favorite sayings is, "The grass isn't greener over there. It's greener where you water it. If the grass is greener over there, I bet the water bill is a lot higher." Take what you have right in front of you and analyze it.

See what's working and what's not, then cultivate more of what is good in your life.

IF YOU CONTINUE TO LIVE IN THE PAST, YOUR LIFE WILL BE HISTORY

"We must look at our disappointments and see what they're really telling us. They usually tell us more than what the disappointments are about."

—MICHAEL A. SINGER

Walking in faith requires you to be active. I wasn't going to find purpose, have committed execution, build my confidence, or achieve something extraordinary sitting down or by focusing only on making money. I needed to stand up and work on the other pillars of my life because being passive does not lead to a neutral state of being. It leads to things getting worse. In life, you're either getting better, or you're getting worse.

I'm starting to realize the setbacks in my past had a huge impact on the story I've been telling myself. When a boss fired me, it created a fear of getting fired again, which led to a distrust of bosses I worked for in the future. When I got dumped, that breakup negatively affected new relationships I formed because I carried that fear of rejection forward. I got dumped a few times, and that hurt, but looking back, I probably deserved it. I could have and should have done better.

I know now that I'm in control of how my past impacts my future. When I carry around disappointments from previous setbacks, the story I tell myself becomes a self-fulfilling prophecy. I realized I was saddled with disappointment, which is dangerous because it didn't allow me to move forward as cleanly and effectively as I should. Disappointment can suck me into a black hole that's difficult to escape from and makes me question everything.

I've learned that you have to move past disappointment, which starts with understanding where disappointment originates. Our ego creates disappointment when it sets up expectations that aren't met. It's that simple. When something bad happens to us, disappointment doesn't flow directly from that bad thing. It flows from the fact that our expectations won't be met now that the bad thing has happened. **There's what we think we deserve and expect, and then there's what the world gives us. The gap in between is disappointment.** If you want to be happier, you must avoid judgment or expectations and give up the need to know what happens tomorrow. That's where you insert faith.

Getting fired sucks not just because you lost your job but because your hopes of being a VP at that company have been dashed. Everyone hates getting dumped because we lose our partner, but what really stings is losing the future we'd envisioned with that person.

Moving on from that disappointment means examining why we experienced the setback that crushed our expectations. If it's a relationship, it's possible you and your partner just weren't right for each other and the breakup was inevitable. When you think about it, do you really want to have a relationship with the wrong person? If you got fired, it could be because you just sucked at your job. You might have gotten so focused on the future and what you hoped to accomplish that you neglected to do the work now.

I remember the sting of disappointment back in 1983 when I got fired from my dream job at the Hyatt, a job where I thought I was on the road to stardom. I called my mother hoping for some sympathy and support.

"Ma, can you believe this hotel?" I asked her. "What they did to me was just wrong!"

"Brandon, Hyatt is a hot, upcoming company," she told me. "They're not in the business of firing good people who can help them. You got fired because you have some flaws in your game that need improvement. Look at this as a chance to get better."

I went into this conversation looking for a shoulder to cry on, and my mother was having none of it. She taught me an important lesson that day. When disappointment strikes, be grateful for the opportunity to reflect and learn from that experience.

It wasn't easy advice to hear in that moment, but I quickly realized that my mom was right. I had some rough edges that I needed to smooth out, so I bought some books and learned how to be a stronger communicator and to better respect authority. It was an eye-opening experience for me and one that was pivotal in how my career unfolded.

REPLACING DISAPPOINTMENT WITH GRATEFULNESS

"Don't carry your mistakes around with you. Instead, place them under your feet and use them as stepping stones to rise above them."

—MICHAEL A. SINGER

I was a young kid when disappointment struck, though. I didn't have the life experience to understand how gratitude in disappointment could help me grow into a person capable of moving forward and achieving great things in the future. As we get older, it should be easier to replace disappointment with gratitude, but that's not always the case.

I have a friend named John who's an incredibly talented, diligent surgeon. He gets into work early and leaves late. He's all-in with his patients and has helped thousands of people improve their health. He's one of those people who puts good into the world every day. However, that commitment came at a cost to John's health in the form of a heart stent in his fifties. All those sixty-hour workweeks, vending-machine meals, takeout meals, short nights of sleep, and missed workouts had caught up to him in a very real and scary way.

We were out for a walk when John told me about it. While he seemed to be in relatively good spirits, he was clearly disappointed and scared that this setback had happened to him.

"I know having a stent put in is scary, but let's look at the positives here," I told him. "I think God sent you a message. You didn't get the massive heart attack because you've done a lot of good for other people. You got the wake-up call instead. There's more good work for you to do, but you can only do it if you start taking better care of yourself."

I was trying to help John realize that life's disappointments don't happen to you—they happen for you. He saw the stent as a setback. In reality, it was an incredible opportunity for him to reset his life and discover a new purpose. After prioritizing the health of his patients over his own for years, he now had a chance to focus on improving his own health for the purpose of serving his patients at a high level for years to come.

It's important to realize you can't have a "Why did this happen to me?" attitude. I would say to that, "Who's it supposed to happen to?" Life's not about what happens to us, it's about what we do with it.

I had to introduce the airplane rule to John—in the event of an emergency, first take care of yourself, then take care of others. We talked about a plan to create a more optimistic future by turning the bad habits into good habits. Instead of getting into the office every morning at 6:00 a.m., he would get into work an hour later two days a week so he could work out at a nearby gym. He committed to working out on the weekends, since he didn't have to travel into the city. His secretary started ordering healthy food and snacks for him so he didn't have to raid the vending machine after operations.

His initial plan had been to "eat better and work out more often." I knew from experience that kind of half-hearted approach wouldn't cut it. We created a lifestyle game plan for John that would allow him to achieve his purpose (something we'll cover in Chapter 8).

Before we did that, I had to help my friend shake off the fog of disappointment so he could make something good out of his new situation. I tried to be a little nicer than my mom was to me, but I had to show him some tough love so he heard the message loud and clear. "Disappointment doesn't happen to you. It happens for you."

ONE WAY TO BUILD FAITH EVERY DAY

"Stop being afraid of what could go wrong and start being excited of what could go right."

—TONY ROBBINS

Along the way, I've learned to find the fractures in my story, forgive my mistakes, and build my self-confidence in all areas of life. I saw these were great ways to strengthen my faith, but I know they can seem a little daunting if you're struggling to let go of fear. If you need to break these strategies down into something more manageable, here's my favorite and my day-to-day goal: just beat yesterday.

That's it. Just do better today than you did yesterday.

I like the way one of my friends, a real estate mogul, said it when we were eating lunch together a while back. He told me he woke up on his twenty-seventh birthday and realized this was the year he'd enjoy his ten thousandth day on this planet. (I never thought about it that way.)

He started to wonder if he was looking at the wrong metric when measuring how old he was. Instead of looking at years, should he be looking at days? That's what my friend chose to do. On top of that, he wanted to get a little smarter by learning two things every day.

If he learned two things every day, by the time he got to his twenty thousandth day, he'd have all the answers he needed when challenges arose, or he'd know where to find the answers.

My friend understands what it means to beat yesterday. He knows that an extraordinary life isn't built in a day, but he makes sure he's working on building it every day.

That's what it's all about—slow and steady growth. I didn't go from a poor diet to eating healthy in one day. I had to start slow and try eating one healthy meal a day. Even now, I'm not perfect. I eat twenty-eight meals a week, and despite my best efforts, I'm not going to eat twenty-eight healthy meals. Can I go twenty-two and six, though? (I think that kind of record would win the division in baseball.)

Give yourself the same grace. My older brother used to ask me, "How do you eat a big, white elephant? One bite at a time." Set up what I like to call "snackable goals" on the way to the finish line. If you eat one or two healthy meals a week, can you improve to three meals this week and then four by next week? Within a month, can you have a healthy meal every day?

I decided to be more engaged with my family and started by being more engaged with my kids, which meant having one more conversation with them this week than I did last week. I asked myself, *Can I schedule one more date with my wife this month than I did last month? Can I take one more family vacation this year than I did last year?*

I like to say that Rome wasn't built in a day, but they were working on it every day.

You don't need to be an overnight success to achieve something extraordinary. You just need consistent execution of a strategy designed to move you closer to your goal every day. It's simple, but it's not easy. I realized I get a little crazy with my schedule, so I needed to start scheduling the date night with my wife or time with my kids instead of just hoping those things would happen. It all starts with believing that you've been placed here with a purpose and developing the faith needed to pursue that purpose with commitment.

If you need to build your faith, don't overcomplicate it. Just beat yesterday, and you'll find your faith increases as you accomplish those snackable goals along the way.

I had to remind myself that you can't experience faith and fear at the same time, so I started choosing faith over fear, and things started to soar.

CHAPTER 2

FILL YOURSELF, FORGET YOURSELF

"The meaning of life is to find your gift. The purpose of life is to give it away."

—PABLO PICASSO

Every morning when I go to work, I try to think of two people I can help with a random act of kindness. I may send someone a book, a handwritten note (taking out a piece of paper and a pen, for the young ones), or a piece of sports memorabilia. I might write a check for a random charity or cause. I might help somebody get a job. It doesn't have to be a huge gift or a lot of money, just something positive for someone who's not expecting it.

On days when I'm not feeling my best, these random acts of kindness are hugely uplifting. My day always improves when I do something for someone else. I don't parade it around when I help someone, either. I'm not looking for accolades. I just want to lift that person up and make their day better. In the process, I know my day will improve, as well.

I give talks all over the country, and this point always resonates with those in the audience. I'll have people follow up with me shortly after my presentation and say they did acts of kindness for a couple people and it completely transformed their day. The next line is usually something to the effect of, "I'm going to start doing this all the time!"

They've discovered, like myself and many others have, that to fill yourself, it's best to forget about yourself and concentrate on helping others. Not only does it infect you with positive feelings, it seeps into the lives of those you help and inspires them to pay that kindness forward to others. You can make the world a better place just by showing kindness to people every day. What an amazing opportunity we have!

I often see wealthy people near the end of their lives doing a huge amount of charity work. I wonder if it's because they don't want to die with all the money they've accumulated, or because they're hoping it gives them a lift to where they're going after this life. I'm reminded of the NBA games I watch frequently. It doesn't seem like a lot of action is happening until the fourth quarter. While it's never too late to start helping others, why wait so long?

I've always felt that helping people brings me the highest level of joy. If you wait until the end of your life to make the world a more joyful place, you're missing out on something incredible. It's like focusing on your fitness. You want to work out and improve your health before you land in the hospital with arthritis or illness, not afterwards.

People tend to postpone doing good with their wealth because it doesn't show up on a profit-and-loss statement. Speaking as a businessperson, I admit that too many of us focus on line items, but it's the stuff that falls below the line that makes the biggest impact.

This was a big realization I had after I sold the company. I had been so concerned with doing well that I didn't do enough good. Now my focus is on doing as much good as I can, the by-product of which is usually me doing well.

The next time you're planning your day, commuting to work, or enjoying lunch, pick out two people you know and think of something positive you can say or do for them. On top of making someone's day better, I guarantee you'll find yourself brimming with positive energy, thoughts, and emotions. Before long, you'll be looking to do it every day.

WHAT WOULD YOU DO FOR SOMEONE WHO COULDN'T DO ANYTHING FOR YOU IN RETURN?

"The game of life is a game of boomerangs. Our thoughts, deeds and words return to us sooner or later with astounding accuracy."

—FLORENCE SCOVEL SHINN

Part of being extraordinary means helping others realize the extraordinary potential in their lives. It's about adding value to the world by doing something for someone that they can't do for themselves. If you live with faith, you're not worried about getting anything in return because you realize the kindness you're showing will come back around to you at some point, whether in this life or the next.

I've learned that when you put out good, you get back good. I've seen how finding your purpose and combining it with commitment and passion makes you unstoppable. Helping others makes you unstoppable too. Many people have discovered this truth on their way to founding amazing companies. Think about the shoe company, TOMS, that donates a pair of shoes to children in need for every pair that's purchased.

You can't fake a genuine love and concern for other people. Just because a boss goes around slapping everyone on the back and saying, "Great job," doesn't mean he gives a crap about the well-being of his employees. People know when you care about them. I'm not the most celebratory boss in the world, but the people who work for me know that I see the good in them and I'm grateful for the positive traits they bring to the table.

I used to take people for granted, especially if I'd been in a relationship with them for a long time. I had to start pausing to show gratitude and appreciation to the people I care about for what they bring to my life. Doing so keeps my relationships from stagnating.

I've always tried to show gratitude to the people that help me, but the importance of gratitude and showing it to people hit me like a ton of bricks when a friend of mine, Barry Watkins, invited me to his "slow-down party." There were about three hundred of us at this party, and we were all wondering the same thing: *What the hell is a slow-down party?*

I thought it might be Barry's idea of a retirement party. After an incredible thirty-year career doing some amazing things for Madison Square Garden, perhaps he was going to announce his plans to scale back his workload and spend more time with family. That was part of it, but as Barry explained, he wasn't retiring. He was refiring his life by creating a list of new *whys* and pursuing them with a renewed commitment and passion.

In order to do that, you have to start with gratefulness and appreciation for everything you've been able to experience. Barry had called us all to this party to show gratitude for what we'd brought in his life up to that point. What can happen after thirty years in a long and successful career is that the more important things can get pushed to the side—your spouse, kids, health, and more. What I took away from Barry's party was that I needed to go back and make sure I wasn't backordered on my "I love you's" and my "Thank you's."

After this party, one thing that became very important to me was finding something good to say to my wife every day—"I love your hair." "I love your shoes." "I love how hard you work." I've been married thirty years and have seen my wife in every dress she owns plenty of times. But if the dress looks good and so does she, why not tell her?

It's all about having those touch points throughout the day, which is a concept I learned from the book *Men Are from Mars, Women Are from Venus* by John Gray. In that book, Dr. Gray offers another piece of advice I took to heart: "Don't buy your wife a dozen roses. Buy her one rose a dozen times." Again, it's about daily touch points, not occasional ones.

When was the last time you did something great for your wife? For your kids? For your employees? When you do that, it shows them how much you appreciate them.

I've found that consistently thinking about someone other than myself is a great way to grow my faith because it forces me to have a more positive perspective. When I see the good in people, I understand why they're worth my attention and effort, which gives me the desire to help them. The world looks a lot better with this outlook.

An effective way of lifting yourself above that fear is to look for the good in others. Doing so shifts your focus from the negative to the positive, allowing your faith to grow.

FOCUS ON THE POSITIVES

In my younger years, I was not a guy who focused on the positives. Put it this way: I used to go to Rockefeller Center when they lit the Christmas tree. Instead of focusing on the 45,000 beautiful lights strung across the tree, I'd find the four lightbulbs that were out.

At work, I used to ask employees to complete ten tasks,

and when they were done, I'd harp on them for the one task they did worst on, not the nine tasks they did well.

I've realized now that's a terrible way to live life. At the very least, it's probably not the way to live a long and happy life. Speaking of, I recently read a blog post in which a woman in her late nineties shared three tips for living a long life:

1. Be happy with where you are.
2. Exercise often and eat clean.
3. Find the good in people every day.

It was interesting to me that finding the good in people was one of her top tips for living a long life, but as I continued reading, it made more sense. We're all guilty of spending too much time thinking about people's bad characteristics. Each of us have good qualities that are worthy of recognition. For some folks, those qualities may be harder to find. It's at times like these we need to go beneath the surface and find the good in people.

I love this example the woman shared during the interview: "I had a boss I absolutely hated. However, I saw the way he treated his son when he visited the office, and I knew he was a good father. Whenever I thought of him, I didn't get caught up in the kind of boss he was or how he treated his employees. I just always thought of him as a good dad."

It's easy to focus on imperfections, but unless we take a walk in someone's shoes, we don't know all the things going on in their lives. Leave the judgment for the person upstairs.

I've seen this with a bunch of ineffective coaches who walk into a huddle during a timeout or in practice and start ripping their players a new one. As a player, would you be motivated to play for a coach who constantly pointed out your shortcomings? If you were a pro, maybe, but you wouldn't be happy about it.

If you're a manager, you can look for the positives when talking to employees about their performance. I'm not just talking about annual reviews here. If somebody works for me, I want them to know what I'm thinking. When sharing my thoughts, I keep it simple: **"Here are the things I want you to do more of, and here are things I want you to do less often."** I always lead with the positive, then give constructive feedback.

TRADE YOUR EXPECTATIONS FOR APPRECIATION

It was February 15, 2018, and the Washington men's basketball team had fallen in double overtime to Utah, a loss which gave the team a three-game losing streak. Coach Mike Hopkins and his players were getting frustrated. Before the losing streak, they'd compiled an impressive 18-6 record. At 18-9, disappointment was starting to creep in.

After staying up past midnight watching the game on my iPhone in bed, I texted Mike the next morning with some advice. I'd met Mike during his time at Syracuse and had been mentoring him for over twelve years, and now he was the Washington head coach.

One thing I noticed during the game that I shared in that text was that Mike's players looked miserable at halftime despite the fact that they were winning. As I watched the camera pass from one Washington player to the next before the half, I saw zero smiles. This was their demeanor when they had the halftime lead. Imagine if they had been losing!

In essence, I advised Mike that it was time to hit the pause button with his team. They'd gotten too focused on the individual stuff and lost sight of the team's goals. In outperforming expectations, they were starting to buckle under the weight of being expected to win games.

I suggested to Mike it was time for his team to trade their

expectations for appreciation. If I had told them before the season that they'd be 18-9 after twenty-seven games, everyone on the team would've signed up for that. It was time to look at what they'd accomplished and not focus on the losing streak. To do that, they didn't need a grueling practice or hours spent in the film room reliving their mistakes.

They needed to go see a movie as a team and eat some pizza.

Mike's response made me laugh. He said something to the effect of, "I'm uncomfortable doing that now. It doesn't feel like the right time to do this. I'm trusting you here."

He arranged for a shuttle to take the players to see *Black Panther* and get some pizza afterwards. It was like magic. Mike texted me later to thank me for encouraging the reset with his players. He said they were looser and more energetic during the next practice. His team was no longer down in the dumps. They had a little extra spring in their step.

It carried over the rest of the season, as the Huskies won three of their last five games, won a game in the National Invitation Tournament, and finished 21-13. Mike won Coach of the Year in the Pac-12. It was a great turnaround from last season's 9-22 finish.

Most of us don't have game tape to watch after a day at the office, but if we did, what would we see? Someone who's smiling and working happily, or someone with a sourpuss look?

I have to remind myself that we all have good in our lives, even if it's hard to find sometimes. When I find positive traits and focus on them, it's a great way to reset myself, motivate others, or change the negative views I have about someone. I read recently that humans have about 60,000 thoughts per day. If I can infuse a few thousand of those with more positivity, it will change how I view the world and how I impact those around me.

Positive thoughts bring light into the world, and we could all use a little more of that.

TAKE INVENTORY OF YOUR RELATIONSHIPS

The four things that matter to me the most in business relationships are:

- Do I trust you?
- Do I really know you?
- Do you understand me?
- Are you what's best for me?

The answers to these four key questions help me take

inventory of my relationships. I used to struggle to find the good in people and didn't extend kindness to as many people as I should. I realized I wasn't surrounding myself with the right people, so one of the things I did was join the Harvey Mackay Roundtable in order to develop some new, positive relationships. It's not easy when you're fifty to make new friends, but I did it.

It's funny. When I talk to friends of mine who run companies, they think of inventory as the number of products on the shelves or the amount of raw materials in the warehouse. These assets are counted, sorted, and qualified. CEOs develop an inventory because it's important to know how many assets they have and what those assets are worth to the company.

What's interesting to me is that when I ask CEOs what their most important asset is, they tell me it's their people, not products or raw materials. Yet they don't treat those assets like all the others and take inventory of their team members. If they did, they'd know the strengths of each employee and could see areas where the company is deficient.

Maybe someone with excellent time-management skills could be given a promotion to manage a department that constantly runs behind on shipping orders. You might have an employee in product development who's floundering because they lack creativity. If you don't take inventory of your team members, you'll never discover these insights.

It's not enough to say people are your most important asset. You've got to act like it.

I take inventory of my relationships on a personal level too. I know that at the end of my life, a big part of my success will be based on the relationships I've had. Successful people take inventory of their relationships to ensure they're surrounded by the best possible people, those whose positive traits rub off on their own lives.

I had to look at the people I shared relationships with and put their characteristics under the microscope. Every relationship is built on communication and trust. Can I talk to that person about anything? Do I trust them? Without those characteristics, it's difficult to have a meaningful relationship. If somebody can tell me I've got a crumb in my teeth, my outfit doesn't suit me, or I'm acting like an asshole, I consider that valuable information.

I value someone who will be my friend regardless of mishaps, who will invest in a long-term relationship that can survive the ups and downs.

One of the most important things I've learned from the

Harvey Mackay Roundtable after seven years is that if you want to become wealthy, the top trait you're looking for in people shouldn't be their wealth. You want people in your life who are smart, kind, loyal, and reliable. The number in someone's bank account doesn't guarantee they'll possess those traits. Sadly, the opposite is often true.

Taking inventory of my relationships showed me I needed to detach from some toxic relationships that were stirring up negative thoughts and emotions. By cutting away these poisonous influences, I was able to build healthier relationships that injected some much-needed positivity into my life. I had to fight with (and in some cases, fire) some friends, neighbors, and even family. It was weird to do it, but I did it.

Taking inventory of my relationships brought my family members, friends, those I worked with, and others to the forefront of my mind. It reminded me of the reasons I cherish those relationships and motivated me to show unexpected kindness to those I love.

BEING KIND AND GENEROUS IS UNDERRATED

"There are three ways to ultimate success: The first way is to be kind. The second way is to be kind. The third way is to be kind."

—FRED ROGERS

I've found as a business leader that treating my clients kindly isn't always easy. In a perfect world, I'd only have to work with outstanding clients, those who provided automatic motivation for my employees because they enjoyed working on those accounts.

The success of my business is determined by the relationships I have with clients, and when the client is easy to work with, the relationship is a breeze.

In our company, we do everything we can to make raving fans out of our clients. We set aside our pride and do the work even when it's thankless. When clients are jerks, we try to focus on their positive attributes. If there are none to be found, we turn our attention to how the deal will help our company grow or sharpen the skills of our employees.

Even with that mindset in place, some clients just don't work out, and we move away from them when possible. It wouldn't be feasible to dismiss every bad client, but we have fired a few. I believe the greatest kindness you can show unhappy clients is to let them go. That way, they're free to pursue a new relationship and so is your company. I realized by moving away from a few bad clients, it opened the door for new, better clients to come in, and it made our company happier.

Besides the client's happiness, you also have to protect the well-being of your employees. After all, you worked hard to recruit, hire, and train them. You've poured countless hours and dollars into making them invaluable parts of your team.

As a manager, one of the traits I know I must possess is talent acquisition. I have to hire the right people and then protect those assets once I bring them onboard. The mistake I made when I was younger was hiring young people who were willing to work for less because they didn't know better. Surprise—they usually didn't do better either.

Lou Holtz is famous for saying, "You know how you get the best people working for you? Just get rid of all the bad ones." There's some truth to that.

One of my biggest mistakes over the years was not firing certain people sooner or failing to be tough on people I knew didn't fit into our organization.

I used to feel bad about firing people. Now I don't because it's as much a help to me and the company as it is to them. Why would you want to work for a company if you're not all-in for them, if you're not going to be dedicated to helping the company grow?

Life's short. Nobody should waste forty-plus hours each

week doing something that is not their purpose. Some people don't see that, and as a manager, you've got to help them see it, even if it's not convenient. That's what it means to be kind in the workplace.

CHAPTER 3

RELATIONSHIPS THAT WIN

"You have people who love you and people who hate you. Focus on them. The people who are indifferent (in the middle)—leave them out of it."

I woke up one day and realized many of my relationships had changed. I guess I got caught up with growing my business. I also got caught up in the way things used to be, so when change happened, I experienced deep disappointment in my relationships. I think this happens with all of us. The friend we used to see every week has a kid and can only hang out occasionally. The job performance of a once-reliable employee begins to slip because they're going through a divorce. A child leaves for college and doesn't call home as much anymore.

We have to adjust when our relationships change if we want to keep them. We can't get caught up in our expectations for the relationship. Instead, we should be grateful for what others can realistically and honestly give.

Winning relationships are important, but like anything worthwhile, they take work to cultivate and keep. Relationships require trust, patience, and two-way communication. I needed to stop being selfish. I like to say that success starts when selfishness ends. I needed to adopt more of a selfless mentality to be a better spouse, parent, friend, coworker, and boss.

The relationships in my life had been stymied by the fact my life was consumed with the success Steiner Sports was enjoying and with maintaining our newfound status. In the beginning, it was cool, but after a while, those close to me grew bored with talking about my company in every conversation.

Before we get into the specifics of building winning relationships, I think it's important we start at the beginning. How do you begin a winning relationship with someone?

START RELATIONSHIPS OFF ON THE RIGHT FOOT

"A great relationship is about two things. First, find out the similarities. Second, respect the differences."

—UNKNOWN

Every good relationship begins with honesty and the sharing of information. It's important to let the other person know who you are, what you think, and what's important to you. Then, just as important, you need to listen as the other person shares with you. If you bypass this foundation, your relationship will be in rough waters from the start.

Looking only at the surface can get people in trouble when forming new relationships. Think about sports. We've seen plenty of teams bring in big name free agents with great stats who aren't a fit culturally with the team. You need more than in-game production if that new player is going to gel with their teammates. You need an alignment of ideas between the team and the player on what it takes to win. If there's a mismatch, what initially seems like a gain will soon be realized as a failure.

For years, I hired people at Steiner Sports based on their résumé and not their fit with our culture and what value they could bring to the company. As a result, the company often felt unsettled. Employees didn't get along, and there was constant infighting.

Once I started looking past the résumé at what kind of fit the employee would be, I hired the right people, and our company became a much happier place to work.

It takes time, energy, and commitment to form solid relationships. Think about your most important relationships and how much time you spend sharing ideas. If you go on a trip with your boss and spend time together on an airplane or at dinner, there's a good chance your relationship will take off because you're learning about each other.

The same thing happens in sports. When teams go on their first big road trip, it's during the downtime on flights or in hotels that teams usually come together. Sometimes in the work environment, you don't get that. You may sit next to a person day after day but have no idea what they're like. This happens in our schools and neighborhoods too. You have no idea what your neighbor does or anything about the classmates sitting beside you.

In *The Power of Who*, Bob Beaudine says the key isn't necessarily meeting other people, but rather getting to know the people you know and who they know. It's a better way of networking and strengthening your life. Everybody is always trying to get to the next meeting as opposed to paying attention to somebody you already know.

I spoke at a university recently and asked this young lady

what winning looked like to her. She told me she wanted to be a money manager, someone who handled big-time mergers and acquisitions. I pointed at the young man sitting next to her in the auditorium and asked if she knew him. She said they had classes together and were friendly with each other.

"Young man, what does your father do for a living?" I asked him.

"He's in finance," the young man replied. "His company handles mergers and acquisitions."

This young lady was sitting five feet away from a classmate whose father was in the exact line of work she wanted to do one day. A life-changing connection was right under her nose, yet she might never have discovered it because she, like many of us, didn't take the time to learn about someone she saw every day. Get to know the people you know. **It's not who you know or what you know, but what you know about who.**

Great relationships aren't only about what you can do for each other, but helping each other win is important to keeping the relationship going. **People love to surround themselves with people who help them win.** If you're going to help me be a better dad, aid my spiritual initiatives, or contribute to my physical health, you're a winner. I want to keep you around me.

THE TRUTH WILL SET YOU FREE, BUT IT MIGHT PISS YOU OFF AT FIRST

Honesty is another cornerstone of good relationships. Even when it's difficult, you must be able to share the truth with the other person. It might hurt their feelings, but if it comes from a place of love and respect, honesty can always help us grow.

Ottis Anderson is someone who appreciates the role of honesty in a relationship. In many ways, Ottis was my *Jerry Maguire* moment. In the early '90s, I was skidding along, trying everything I could to stay in business. I was doing some work for the New York Giants and, among my many efforts, was trying to book players for appearances.

Recently traded to New York from the St. Louis Cardinals, Ottis had won Rookie of the Year but was currently third on the depth chart behind running backs Joe Morris and Rodney Hampton. We developed a relationship based on our mutual interests. Ottis wanted to raise his profile and make a few bucks, and I was desperate to work with any of the Giants who'd give me a shot. Shortly after we started working together, Ottis found himself thrust into the starting running back role after Hampton got hurt and Morris was cut.

The Giants had a phenomenal year, and Ottis had a lot to do with the team's success. Before the conference championship against the San Francisco 49ers, I called Ottis and told him I wouldn't be coming to the Super Bowl if they won against the 49ers. Instead, I would stay back in New York and work my ass off getting appearances lined up for Ottis.

"Brandon, I had a dream that we beat the 49ers and then won the Super Bowl," Ottis told me. "Not only did we win the game, but I was named Super Bowl MVP!"

"If that happens, I just need you to call me and stay in touch," I replied.

It was a moment for both of us to exercise a little faith. The Giants were underdogs against the 49ers, and even if they won, Ottis would be up against several teammates for MVP honors. I chose to have faith not only that this outcome was possible but that Ottis would call me after the two biggest games—and hopefully wins—of his NFL career.

The Giants won the game, then beat the Buffalo Bills in Super Bowl XXV. Just as he had predicted, Ottis won the

MVP award, and suddenly, everyone was vying for his marketing rights. I couldn't match the resources of the larger firms, but I did have a relationship with Ottis from before he was a household name. I prayed that would be enough.

Ottis picked me to represent him and handle his marketing. It was a huge moment for me, as Ottis was one of the first big athletes I signed. A few months after the Super Bowl, I received a call from someone who wanted Ottis to speak in Washington, D.C.

I got the call on Monday, and the speech was to be on Wednesday. It was tight, but I talked Ottis into doing it and booked our travel arrangements. We made our way to Newark International Airport, and as we were about to board the plane, Ottis asked me where we were sitting. I told him with it being last minute, the best I could do was get us seats in the back of the plane. Ottis wasn't happy. He stopped, turned around, and went to exit the plane. But before he did, he got on the microphone (remember, this was 1991 when rules on planes were more relaxed) and shared his displeasure with the crowd.

"I'm the Super Bowl MVP," he told the other passengers. "This guy has us sitting in coach at the very back of the plane. Do you all think he's doing a good job?"

The crowd went wild, and Ottis exited the plane. For the next half hour, I begged him to get on the plane. I didn't know what to do. Just as the flight attendant was about to shut the door, he agreed to board the plane.

During the entire flight, he kept saying, "I can't believe you got us in coach."

I'd just been through thirty minutes of hell, and I was worn out.

We did the appearance and headed back to New York. As we were driving home, he said something to me that totally changed my approach in this business.

"I'm busting your balls because you're young and trying to break into this business, and I want you to understand that how you treat players has a profound effect on us," he said. "You're my guy, so I'm telling you this for your own good, so you can build a business.

"Number one, you've got to pay the players up front. You can't expect us to do all this work and hope we'll be paid. That's not how it works in the professional player business. If you pay up front, we will always show up because we know we're getting paid.

"Secondly, the accommodations and transportation must

be first class. You can't just pick me up in your Ford Mustang. You've got to get a car service. You've got to fly us first class. We're bigger, taller, and we need more space. You can't expect us to sit in coach."

Looking back on it, Ottis was trying to get my attention because I was stubborn. I used the excuse that money was tight and I couldn't afford the car and first-class plane tickets. But in reality, that was the business I wanted to be in, so I needed to figure it out.

Being able to share the truth with each other is the sign of a good relationship. Ottis was brutally honest with me, and because I kept my ego in check, I learned so much from him that day. Twenty-five years later, I still have that relationship with Ottis. That's what I appreciate about him. I was at a critical juncture, and his words made a major impact on me. When I followed his advice, players didn't balk at working with me.

STARTING AND STRENGTHENING RELATIONSHIPS

One of my biggest strengths when it comes to starting relationships is that I focus on helping somebody solve a problem or serving somebody in an unconditional way. When I want to get a relationship started with somebody, the first thing I think of is, *How can I help them with their charity? How can I help them with their kids?* Helping someone with what's important to them is an effective relationship starter.

But it's only a starter. I can't just show up and help one time. It's a continued effort and requires caring. I don't expect favors in return. I don't track things like that because it's playing small when you do. My mantra is, "Do as much as you can, for as many people as you can, as often as you can, and expect nothing back."

I made a list of the people that it would be amazing if I got a chance to meet them, and then I started working on how to meet them. These were people who could help me change my health or my business, plus people I just thought it would be cool to hang out with socially. I started to make new friends and form new relationships. At age forty-five, that's not easy!

When you want to meet somebody, it's important not to use just anyone to introduce you. Sometimes people will stretch out of their comfort zone to make an introduction, then suddenly, the person to whom you're being introduced is wondering what the premise of the introduction is. You need to meet people on the right premise.

My mother always said, "If you want to get to somebody and you can't get to them directly, get to somebody who's really important to them." There's a big difference between finding somebody who's important to that person versus somebody who *says* they know them.

As a relationship begins, the first thing I ask myself is, *What value can I bring to the person?* Most people focus on what they can get from someone, but I always try to think about what I can do for the other person regardless of whether it will help me or not.

When I start a relationship, I want the other person to know two things: "I see you," and "I'm here for you." I try to have this kind of relationship with all my friends, family, and employees too. They know I see them, I know their situations, and I'm there for them.

I asked our therapist once, "What's the big deal to my kids if I get home every night? They're in high school now. Often when I'm home, they don't talk to me."

The therapist replied, "Knowing you're right outside their door and available in case they need something is very meaningful. That's what makes parents so significant, even to the day they die. Kids can make that phone call and know their parents will pick up."

I realized if I wanted to have more friends and better friendships, I needed to be a better friend. People you want to have a relationship with need to know you care for them.

I've found it helps to start as many relationships as I can. My son, Crosby, likes to say, "We can't meet enough people." I understand that not every relationship will be as meaningful as others, but I also know that to have more of them, you must start more of them. Even if the relationship isn't long term, you can be grateful for the time you spent with that person and what you learned from them.

When did they develop a cut-off age for making new friends? They say as you get older, it's harder to make new friends. "You can't teach an old dog new tricks" is the saying I hear all the time. I hate that saying because it's not true. An old dog can learn new tricks if they're properly motivated, which means you can make new friends no matter your age. It just takes effort. You've got to walk across the street and say hello to somebody or ask a couple questions to the office mate next to you.

In my case, I flew across the country four times a year for the Harvey Mackay Roundtable to spend quality time with my new friends and learn more about them. Many of them have now been to my house, and I've been to theirs. I've developed some great relationships from that roundtable.

RELATIONSHIP RENEGOTIATION

I had to renegotiate a lot of my relationships after selling Steiner Sports. At work, two of my most important employees, ones who'd helped me build the company, suddenly didn't see the value of continuing to work together. They were filled with fear instead of faith, which caused them to miss the upside of this renegotiated relationship I was offering. In the end, they decided to leave the company they'd help build, which was heartbreaking for me.

At home, I also had to renegotiate my marriage. Before selling the company, I worked first, worked second, worked third, and whatever time was left over, that's what Mara and I would enjoy. How I prioritized my time had to change. I also committed to talking less about Steiner Sports when we were together, whether it was at home or out with friends.

Sharing information and setting expectations are essential ingredients in successful relationships. If either, or both, of these ingredients suddenly dry up, a relationship that was once strong and vibrant can turn sour. That's what happened to me while I was working to build my business, and when I called the timeout to reassess how my life was going, I saw relationships that had changed, but I hadn't changed with them. I'd neglected them, and now I was facing a lot of renegotiation to make them healthy once again.

I used to be tempted to end relationships when they took a turn for the worse, whether that meant firing a once-reliable employee or refusing to answer the phone when a wayward friend called me out of the blue. When the flow of information dried up and my expectations were no longer being met, it seemed like my only option was to cut that person out of my life.

Now I practice relationship renegotiation to repair strained or broken relationships instead of just ending them. I learned about this concept at John Dewey High (then an experimental school) in a class called "Group Dynamics," and it stuck with me.

Frank Bisignano, CEO of First Data, loves to say, "The circumstances have changed." When the circumstances of my relationship change, I have to change with them by coming together with the other party and renegotiating the "terms" of our relationship. I don't draw up a contract or anything like that. Rather, I sit down with the other person to exchange new facts, ideas, and expectations to get a better idea of where we both are.

I've talked to couples that say they've both changed, and they seem distraught by this idea. My response is always, "Did you think you would stay the same for forty years? Why not understand the change you've both undergone, adapt to it, and make the most of it?"

If a relationship I share with someone is important to both of us, we owe it to each other to have this conversation. To expect things to never change is insane, and I've learned that jumping ship rather than working things out is lazy. The same is true when we take relationships for granted. Relationships require effort, and renegotiating them is a great opportunity to put that belief into practice.

A quote above my desk reads, "Life is a series of compromises and adjustments." If I can't compromise or adjust when my relationships change, I won't have many of them left.

My wife and I are experiencing change now, as none of our kids live in town anymore. We're figuring out how to renegotiate those relationships without disrupting their lives. We've realized we won't get the same level of interaction with our kids that we're used to, so we're trying to adjust and remain grateful for the time we do get to spend with them on the phone or in person. As parents of grown kids, that's all we can do.

My mother-in-law was preemptive in this regard. She negotiated the relationship my wife and I would have with them before we were even married! She wasn't too worried about the details of the wedding, which many mothers focus on. She was playing the long game, and

she was worrying about the most important thing—
our relationship.

"Good agreements prevent disagreements."

—HARVEY MACKAY

"I have just two things I want to ask of you," she told me.
"First, I'd like to be able to call my daughter any time.
Second, when you have kids, will you bring them to see
us in Florida?"

As a businessman, I appreciated her direct negotiation
style, and as her future son-in-law, I loved that she was
so passionate about having a relationship with us and our
future kids. I assured her that she could call 24/7 and that
we'd bring the kids down to Florida to visit as much as
we could. She was also welcome to visit us in New York
whenever she wanted.

Another great example happened at work. One of my best
salespeople quit unexpectedly, and when I asked him why,
he said he couldn't make the commute anymore. Rather
than letting him quit with no objection, I took a stab at
relationship renegotiation.

I asked him, "If I let you come in and leave earlier so you
miss the traffic, will you stay?" He said he would, and
he's been with the company four years since that day. His

commute time was cut in half, and we kept a valuable member of our team.

FACING THE STRUGGLE OF FORGIVENESS

"If you burn your neighbor's house down, it doesn't make your house look any better."

—LOU HOLTZ

I discovered I was carrying a lot of anger and held many grudges. There were people in every area of my life I hadn't spoken to in years. This was especially true in business, where, let's be honest, shit happens sometimes. I came to see that it didn't matter if I was right or wrong in those situations. What mattered was whether I could find my way to mercy and forgiveness with people in business, my friends, and even family members.

A lot of people have told me they don't care about letting go of anger or resolving grudges they have. I didn't want to live the rest of my life carrying that baggage. If I'm going to be here a while, I decided to take care of that stuff ASAP. The process didn't play out overnight, but I made those phone calls to offer forgiveness, show mercy, or apologize.

Some relationships I was able to make healthy again, while others were too far gone. Just because I was ready to restore the relationship or resolve the hurt didn't mean the other party was ready. That wasn't the point, though. It was good for me to let go of that anger, release the bad energy I felt, and make things right the best I could.

We've all struggled at times with showing mercy to someone who messed up or hurt us. We'd rather see them get what they deserve—pain and suffering—than give them what they don't. I think this impulse is shared by our society at large. We used to be a forgiving country where people stood up and owned up. Now look at our jails. Look at the way we punish people and fire people. It's become an eye-for-an-eye culture.

I truly feel we're all better than our worst mistake, and we've all made mistakes. We've all done things we're not proud of, and things we wish we could take back. In those moments when we're tempted to withhold mercy and let the other person suffer, I find it helps to remember that we've needed mercy in the past and will need it again in the future. With that in mind, shouldn't we model the behavior we hope to receive?

I like how Oprah defines forgiveness: "Forgiveness is giving up the hope that the past could be different. It's accepting the past for what it is and using the moment to help you move forward." Too often, we let disappointment keep us from moving forward. Failing to let go of that disappointment not only kills the relationship but drags us down into a negative headspace and makes us less trusting of others because we're scared to get hurt again.

When you hold on to being angry with someone—a form of disappointment—you're doing yourself as much a disservice as the person who wronged you.

"When you hold on to your history you do it at the expense of your destiny."

—T.D. JAKES

If you make a mistake, admit it and own it. Make yourself worthy of receiving mercy from someone, but don't expect it. That's what I had to do with Phil Rizzuto, the Hall of Fame Yankees shortstop, after the check I gave him for an appearance bounced. He called me up and chewed my ass, saying we'd never work together again. Panicked, I hustled over to my bank on Madison Avenue and asked my banker why he bounced Phil's check.

"Well, there were two checks that were overdrafted," he explained.

"But why would you bounce Phil Rizzuto's?" I demanded, totally dumbfounded.

"Well, the other check was for Mickey Mantle," he replied.

"Okay," I said, "good choice."

I called Phil, owned up to my mistake, and promised to make things right. This was in the late '80s, and at that time, Phil wasn't a Hall of Famer. I spent a lot of time finding work for Phil and campaigned hard for him to get into the Hall of Fame. He got into the Hall in 1994 via the Veterans Committee and gave one of my favorite induction speeches of all time.

Years later, he ended up telling me, "I've got to give you credit, Brandon. After that stupid blunder with the check, you focused in on me and made me a lot of money. I'm really grateful." I was grateful Phil stuck with me after I let him down. Having a Yankees Hall of Famer was a game changer for my company. I wouldn't have blamed him for cutting ties with me after I bounced his check, but instead, he chose to extend mercy.

I'm not saying you should turn the other cheek in every instance. What I would encourage you to do is examine your life to see if there is someone you've written off who might be deserving of mercy. If there is, take that courageous first step and forgive them for whatever happened in the past. Let go of the disappointment and move forward.

Not only will the other person be grateful for your decision, I think you will be too.

ALEX RODRIGUEZ SEEKS REDEMPTION

Alex Rodriguez called me on Halloween night in 2014. I'll never forget it. I've dealt with Alex before, and he's never randomly called me like that, especially since this was the October after he had been suspended. Come to find out, Alex was seeking redemption for letting down the MLB, his team, his teammates, coaches, and fans, and he wanted my help to win back those he'd disappointed.

I listened as he told me, "I've embarrassed my teammates and my friends. I screwed up with the Yankees, one of the best teams in any sport, and I've got to fix it. Do you think you can help me? I want to come back better and stronger than ever."

I'll admit that I was hesitant at first. I hadn't known a player who screwed up as badly as he did—getting suspended for performance-enhancing drugs on the highest profile team in a year they barely missed the playoffs—who made it back aboveground. Most of the players who messed up like that never stepped foot on a major league field again. Then there was the question of whether Alex could still play coming off hip surgery.

I wasn't sure he could do it, but I was curious enough to keep asking questions. I wanted to know what Alex planned to do differently if he got a second chance.

"I've been working my tail off this off-season, and I'm going to continue working my tail off starting in spring training," he said. "However, I want it to be more than making the biggest comeback of all time on the field. I want it to be a big comeback off the field too. I want to better my relationships off the field too."

I had fallen out of my chair about four times by this point. This was so unlike the Alex I'd known. I told him, "I just want you to understand one thing. If I do help you, you're going to have to listen and do the things I say."

He gave his word that he would listen.

When he went back to spring training, I told him we needed to do a sit-down and tell the world what he was thinking and feeling in an honest, authentic way. It took several months to get him ready to sit in front of eight hundred people at the Hudson Theatre in New York City on November 6, 2015. When he sat down in front of that crowd, he totally owned up to what he did. Here's an excerpt of what we talked about that night:

Alex: I cannot begin to describe how dark those days were.

I created this incredible hole for myself. You wish you could blame the advisors and the lawyers, but at the end of the day, I had to look myself in the mirror and realize that this is on me. I'm the quarterback of this team. I put this team together. I made every decision, and they were brutal, ugly decisions. It's on me. I have to own it. Once I took full control and responsibility of all my poor decisions, then I thought the healing process began.

Brandon: You seem a little emotional about that. Was that an emotional time for you when you were going through that?

Alex: I think when I look back five years from now, I would say that the whole Biogenesis scandal is singlehandedly the greatest thing that ever happened in my life. It gave me an opportunity to take stock into my life, to look in the mirror, and realize that you are responsible and accountable for everything you do, every decision you make, and that's important. But the other thing, Brandon, that I thought, was no matter what I had to face in New York with the media or my teammates, it was the one conversation I had to have with my daughters, about a month before spring training. I thought about this talk for like four months, and I needed four months of waking up and actually rehearsing what I was going to tell my daughters. I broke down, and it was a very emotional talk. I didn't know what they would say. The truth of the matter is if they'd said, "Dad, we want you to stop playing baseball," that would've been it for me.

In addition to the event at the Hudson Theatre, I told him he needed to do something really cool to help somebody in need who had no way of paying him back. We decided to visit an eleven-year-old kid named Jason in Long Island who's a Yankees fan and looks up to Alex. He was also battling cancer at the time. I first went to Jason's house and decorated his room with Yankees gear, then told him we'd go the next day to a game and I'd get him on the field. I never told him he would meet Alex.

The next day, we're at the ballpark hanging out. There's nobody there. All of a sudden, Alex walked into the dugout and tapped Jason on the shoulder. They chatted for a minute, then went onto the field and played catch. When they finished, Alex took Jason into the clubhouse and introduced him to all the Yankees players. It was a very moving experience for all of us.

To help improve Alex's standing with fans and the Yankees organization, we had him do a couple appearances for the Yankees sponsors and some of the season ticket holders. Alex knew he'd screwed up with the Yankees, and he wanted to add value to the organization. He didn't pretend like everything was okay. He worked to help the Yankees and make up for the damage he'd caused with his suspension. He signed autographs at the ballpark before games and brought in a team to help him with PR and TV. During every interview, he focused on his teammates and coaches and moved away from anything he'd done.

"We are continually faced with great opportunities which are brilliantly disguised as unsolvable problems."

—MARGARET MEAD

Alex returned to the game after that and played hard. He focused on being a good teammate and had an amazing year. He showed the kind of person he can be. People had looked at him as a bad person, a cheater, and a guy who disrespected the rules. He showed he could play the game, be a good teammate, and become a good role model. His path back to baseball proves we're all better than our worst mistake. The question is, what will you do with your mistake? Will you run from it or act like it didn't happen? Or will you give people a reason to forgive you?

Mercy and forgiveness don't always come to you when you want them. But when you do the right things consistently, you can move forward in a positive way. You might never get the forgiveness you seek; however, you can lay your head down at night knowing you did everything within your power to repair a fractured relationship. How the other person chooses to respond is up to them. Hopefully one day, they'll extend mercy your way.

Relationships are worth the effort, even when we're asked

to do more than what should be expected of us. Alex's teammates, coaches, and fans didn't have to forgive him after he was suspended. The team could've fired him, and baseball fans everywhere could've written him off as a lying, cheating failure. Many of them chose to fight for that relationship. For those who stuck around, years later, I'm confident they would tell you it was worth it.

PART II

FORTUNE

CHAPTER 4

CAPACITY IS A STATE OF MIND

"You can't be in survival mode and growth mode at the same time."

In the '90s, I lived in Westchester, New York, and took the train into the city for work every morning. I used to joke with people that the only thing I ever caught was my breath. I consistently missed my train and was late for work, and even when I did catch it, I would sit there thinking, *I have to get off this damn train. I hate having to get to work this way. There are no seats. Some people have their shoes off, or they're eating or talking on their phone. It's not a comfortable situation.*

I've had many goals in my life, but in the summer of 1994,

I added a new one: make enough money to buy a car. In my mind, that car represented freedom. I wanted to be free to go to and from work when I pleased and not rely on the train as my method of transportation. It might seem simple, but this was one of the first major purposes I had in my life.

Now I had to figure out how to make enough money to buy that car and get off the train. In June 1994, I found my inspiration. That month, the New York Rangers won the Stanley Cup for the first time in fifty-four years. This was a huge deal for a fan base that felt similar to how Cubs fans felt before their World Series win in 2016—cursed, like everything in the world was conspiring against our team.

The day after they won the title, I squeezed onto the train for my commute. It was hot, the car was packed, and I was immediately miserable. As I looked around at the other passengers, I noticed they were all holding copies of the *Daily News* with Mark Messier's picture splashed across the back cover. In the picture, he was holding the Stanley Cup, and you could tell from his smile that he was the happiest guy in the world.

At this point, my imagination was racing. The Rangers' Stanley Cup win was a unifying moment for New Yorkers, and seeing everyone on the train holding the newspaper with Messier's photo, I got a crazy idea for a commemorative item.

I wanted to take that photo, have Messier sign it, and add the words, "We did it!" I didn't even have a collectible company at that point. My job was to bring athletes around for appearances, store openings, commercials, endorsements, and have them sign autographs. But in that moment, I was confident that if I could get Messier to sign that photo, I could sell 18,000 copies to the diehard Rangers fans who had packed Madison Square to capacity during the regular season and playoffs.

I spent months trying to track Messier down through his sister, brother, accountant, and even his lawyer. Finally, I was able to work out a deal with Messier and hire him as the first spokesperson for Steiner Collectibles, the company I started because of this deal that would later grow to become Steiner Sports. Messier was the talk of the town, and nobody else was doing hockey collectibles at the time. In the end, we sold more than 18,000 signed photos.

A deal that I schemed up on the train helped launch my company and netted me enough money to buy a silver-blue Lexus SC 400. I felt like the richest man in Babylon driving to work in the first new car I'd ever bought. The whole experience rejuvenated me and pushed me to work harder so I could afford more nice things like that car.

People ask me all the time how Steiner Sports got started. I wasn't driven by a grand purpose or the goal to become a millionaire; I just wanted to get off the damn train!

TO PURSUE PURPOSE, YOU MUST BE EFFECTIVE

"You can make more money, but you can't make more time."

—RICK WARREN

I'm starting the fortune section of the book with time management because you have to be efficient to be successful. None of us are sitting around with tons of time on our hands. We have to become experts on managing our capacity effectively. Being poor with time management keeps us from success. It's true that everything starts with purpose, but you can't pursue a new purpose if you're overwhelmed.

When the idea for the signed Messier photo came to me, if I hadn't managed my time well, that idea could've gotten washed away in the grind of daily life. Making that product a reality required a lot of work, which meant I had to be more efficient with my time. I couldn't add five more hours to my day. All I could do was best use the time I was given to develop this idea that started my company down the path to what it's become today.

For a long time, I didn't have a firm grasp on what I

could accomplish in one day. Usually, I overestimated what I could get done, and this false belief caused me to overstuff my schedule, which left tons of forgotten or unfinished items at the end of each day.

I like to use the analogy that these folks are driving a 9,999-pound truck across a bridge with a capacity of 10,000 pounds. Yes, it's technically possible to cross the bridge, but pushing things to the limit is risky behavior that's likely to burn us in the end.

I saw this a lot with my mother, who was working and trying to take care of three kids. She often wasn't home, so she wasn't helping us with our homework. She couldn't go to our games. Her constant stress was a major contributor to her various health problems.

The average person makes thousands of decisions every day. *Should I get up and work out? What should I have for breakfast? What should I wear to work? Should I call my mother? Do I speak up at this meeting or keep quiet? When should I leave to avoid traffic?*

During my reset, I began to simplify my life by making fewer decisions each day. Once I did, I began to see that some of the choices I was putting time and energy into each day were irrelevant. Looking back a week later, I wouldn't care at all what I had for lunch on

Tuesday, so why spend fifteen minutes thinking about it?

These decisions were negatively affecting my relationship with time, which is something my friend Jesse Itzler talks about in his excellent book *Living with the Monks*. Jesse had an epiphany during his time at the New Skete religious community in upstate New York. Here's how he described that realization in a recent interview we did:

> At the monastery, all of the decisions are taken away from you. They tell you when to eat and what they're serving. They tell you where you're going to be for prayer. You wear one outfit. I showered once and never changed. When you have no decisions, and your head isn't bombarded with all of the stuff you have to do, you have so much energy. By about the sixth day, I was so efficient in my thoughts, and so efficient in everything I did at the monastery that I realized I was radically overloaded in my life, and I had to make changes.

I'm not saying we should live in a monastery and eliminate all the decisions we make each day, but I think there's wisdom we can take away from Jesse's experience. The key is to be aware of what's important and how far you can stretch yourself. There are only so many hours in a day and only so many things you can do. When you commit to things you know you won't have time to fit in, you're setting yourself up for disappointment. **The reason people are often miserable is not due to what they're doing but often how much they're doing.** They're involved in too much, leaving no time to actually enjoy anything.

Growing will lead you to happiness, but if you're at capacity, there's no room to grow.

For many years I tried to fit everything in, and I paid the price. I was hungry to build my financial fortune, so I said yes to every opportunity and stayed up long nights to make it happen. I barely remember anything from those years because I rarely slept and was never home, but I know my fortune in other areas of life diminished greatly.

I missed some amazing moments in my family's lives because I didn't manage my time correctly. All I did was rush from one endeavor to the next, some of which I never should have been at in the first place. There were periods of time where I didn't enjoy the work I did or execute it to the fullest extent. I just wanted to check that box and move on to the next one as fast as possible. I was carrying an oversized load across that proverbial bridge every day, which ended in burnout and having to quickly reset my relationship with time.

When I was young, my mother used to tell me, "The problem with you is that you don't have two asses. You can't be in two places at once." She was right, but it wasn't until my forties that I recognized the truth of her words.

Since selling my company, I've learned the power of no and to focus on the most important people, as well as doing the most I can in the least amount of time. I know now that I have to be efficient because I know I can't do everything. I also have to remind myself what's most important in my life and focus on that above everything else. Sometimes that means looking in the mirror and telling myself, "You can't do it all, Brandon." That's not an easy conversation when you're a high achiever like I am. At this point, it's probably a good time to tell you that there's a little Brandon running around inside my head whose had some influence over me throughout the years. When it comes to managing my capacity, Little Brandon tells me I need to do everything. I had to start managing that voice.

I refocused my top priorities and freed up more time for the things I often set aside, like healthy eating and regular exercise. I created an MVP list and a not-to-do list. These lists were game changers for me. Let me tell you, those lists will change your life too.

The first step I took was analyzing my day-to-day life and coming to grips with where I fell on the spectrum. I was doing too much and careening toward burnout.

SATISFACTION STARTS WITH SELF-ANALYSIS

"If you want something you've never had, you must be willing to do something you've never done."

—UNKNOWN

I started paying attention to where I spent my time each day and each week. How much was I doing for whom, when was I doing it, and most importantly, why was I doing it? Was I pursuing my purpose, or was I getting bogged down by distraction and busyness?

When I started looking closely at my schedule, I realized it had been crazy for years, not weeks or months. It was a serious wake-up call for me. I had to accept the fact that I created that insanity myself. It didn't happen to me. I did it, and I had to stop it.

I learned an important lesson as I worked to simplify my schedule: if you've created chaotic circumstances in your daily life, you have the power to change those circumstances for the better. You can't sit back and wait for somebody else to make room on your schedule for what's important because nobody has that power but you. You must be proactive and make the changes yourself; otherwise, it'll never get done.

Keep things simple by focusing on what's most important to you, then build your schedule around that one thing.

For me, what's important is knowing what's going on with my wife and kids and following up on things I need to do with them. I don't want to apologize to them at the end of the day because I didn't get around to them. I can't just say they're my priority. I've got to make sure my actions reflect that statement.

Now when Mara and I go out to dinner a couple times a week (date night), or lunch on the weekends, I leave my cell phone at home. If we're at home eating dinner, I don't take my phone out. I want her to know that she has my undivided attention during that time we're together. The same goes for when I'm eating with my kids. Whatever they want to talk about with me, I'm focused on them. The first time I told Mara I was doing this, I thought she was going to faint.

I can't stress it enough: **leave your cell phone at home on date night!**

We'll talk about my not-to-do list in a moment, but here are some examples of ways I've been able to maximize my time by cutting out certain activities. I don't do early meetings because I work out from seven to eight. I also don't do lunch meetings. A quick sandwich is fine, but I don't need to sit in a restaurant with someone for two hours.

I'm not a good driver, so I minimize my driving time. Not

only that, it costs me money every time I have to drive somewhere because I can't work and drive at the same time. I have someone drive me or ride the train, and I get as much done there as I would at the office. Airplanes have also become an office for me. I'm often on a plane for three or four hours with Wi-Fi and somebody serving me drinks. How can I not be productive?

I don't always examine my schedule and find chaos. Sometimes I see wasted time, which translates to unreached capacity. Should I sit back once in a while and watch my favorite team uninterrupted? Yes. But I shouldn't make a habit of watching game after game without getting anything else done. I was guilty of that for a long time. I watched tons of games and all it did was dumb me down. (Well, maybe I'm still guilty of that.)

This a road to mediocrity. I watch a ton of games, and if I'm at home, I'm probably getting some work done while the game is on. Not always, but a lot of times. When it comes to travel, why wouldn't I use time in an Uber or an airplane to get work done? I'm just sitting there, so it's not like I'm taking away time from my family. I use travel time to go through my emails and touch base with people I haven't talked to in a few months.

The two most important books in your life are your date book and your checkbook—where you spend your time and your money. Most people don't look at their date book that way. I constantly look at my calendar. If I travel to a city for an event, I try to see one or two local clients while I'm there. I'm all about using my time wisely.

What if you look at your date book and find chaos, though? Well, let's start with the first few moments after you wake up and see how to build your day from there.

START THE DAY WITH YOUR MVP LIST

"The most important thing is always the most important thing."

—GARY KELLER

The first ninety seconds of my day set the tone for what happens during the other twenty-three hours, fifty-eight minutes, and thirty seconds. It is during those ninety seconds that I consider two lists that will dictate my actions that day:

- My Most Valuable Priorities (MVP) list
- My not-to-do list

My MVP list is the focus of those first ninety seconds because it speaks to my purpose. It illustrates the important things I should do for the important people in my life.

I don't just use my MVP list to plan my day, though. I

use it to remind myself why I'm working so hard. It's not about the money. It's about using that money to create moments I can enjoy with those closest to me. That's what the MVP list is all about.

I can't forget why I was killing myself in this game of business. I do it for my wife and kids, yet for a long time there, I didn't give them the love, attention, and time they deserved.

I mentioned before that keeping up with my wife and kids is at the top of my MVP list. Exercise is also on there, as is eating healthy meals and snacks during the day. I also prioritize my two acts of kindness. A lot of things can get bumped off my schedule if something unexpected happens, but these items are nonnegotiable.

One of the best things I ever did was to establish Sunday night meetings to plan the week with my wife. She plays mahjong once a week at our house with friends, and I play a pickup basketball game with friends, so we try to match up those nights. If I have a meeting at eight on a Monday night, we'll have dinner together before I go to my meeting. If I have to be away on a particular evening, I make sure she knows ahead of time so she can make plans with friends if she chooses. By taking Sunday to make those plans, I know in the first ninety seconds after I wake up how Mara fits into my day.

I don't want to tell you how to start your day. Some people start with meditation, while others, like me, kick-start their day with a workout. If you're like I was in my younger years, maybe you get out of bed and hit the road right away. Everybody has their own thing, and I respect that. All I'm asking for is the first ninety seconds. Devote those moments to your MVP list, and I promise it'll start your day off in the best possible way.

What you'll find is that when you focus on your top priorities throughout the day, you'll finish the day with as much energy as when you started it. That's because the MVP list allows you to manage your capacity effectively. Rather than cramming every minute with menial tasks, you spread out the important work you need to get done.

A basketball team doesn't employ a full-court press the entire game. They'd be worn out well before the fourth quarter when the game is on the line. They pace themselves in order to have energy when it matters most. Your MVP list allows you to manage your energy throughout the day so you're fresh when you get home, not worn out.

Once I used my MVP to identify my top priorities, it became easier to see the items sucking up my time and making me miserable—those that belong on the not-to-do list.

MAKE YOURSELF A NOT-TO-DO LIST

Most people have a to-do list, but ultimately, your not-to-do list is just as important. Knowing what you don't want to do each day makes tackling your to-do list easier.

There are certain items that should always go on your not-to-do list. I mentioned some of my items earlier. When you think about time-sucking, soul-crushing things that you hate doing, one or more tasks probably jump to mind. Email is a big one for people nowadays. I'll still answer emails, but I much prefer talking to someone on the phone. If you lose hours every day answering emails, put that task on your not-to-do list. Hire a virtual assistant to answer routine emails and text or call you about the important ones.

Is your commute getting your day off to a terrible start? Consider an alternate route, talk to your boss about coming in earlier, take public transportation, or join a carpool. If you still have to endure a long commute, at least you can get some work done while you wait by taking the train or letting someone else drive. That time adds up. Even if your commute is five minutes each way, that's ten minutes a day, which over the course of a year equals 2,400 minutes, or forty hours. That's a full workweek you could put to better use! Many of us don't realize how five minutes every day can add up throughout the year.

Whatever it is that grinds your gears, stop doing it. Put

it on the not-to-do list and free up that time during your day to focus on your MVP list. You'll be happier and more productive.

Whether they mean to or not, certain people suck up a lot of our time. When I see certain names pop up on my caller ID, I'll send them to voicemail unless I have an hour to carve out of my day for them. These needy people should probably land on your not-to-do list most of the time unless you have an open schedule or are feeling abundantly patient.

Sometimes we have to put things on our not-to-do list for our own good or for the good of someone we care about. A friend told me he didn't understand why his marriage wasn't working, so I went over his schedule with him. He did a radio show on Saturdays, played basketball two nights a week with friends, and went to a Syracuse game one night a week. Four nights out of the week, he was totally unavailable to his wife. How could she possibly feel important when he prioritized everything else but her?

If it were me, I'd have cut it down to one night of hoops a week and one or two Syracuse games a month. As much as I love hoops, it would have to go on the not-to-do list for the sake of my wife's happiness. A strong marriage beats basketball any day of the week.

IF YOU NEED HELP, ASK FOR IT

One of the hurdles I faced when trying to implement my MVP list and not-to-do list was making time for my top priorities. One of the best things Mara and I did when we were both working full-time and commuting was to bring in someone to help around the house on Saturdays. Freeing up this time allowed us to run errands, work out, or have a date night. It was a financial sacrifice, but it was totally worth it. We weren't afraid to ask for help because we didn't see it as an indefinite expense. It was a few hours a week if we needed it. Some weeks we didn't need it, but a lot of weeks, we were thankful for that chance to decompress.

You may say you can't afford help, but I say you can't afford not to get help. Being able to have that time for yourself or with your family is always money well spent. It doesn't have to be every week. Getting help even once or twice a month can make a huge difference. Having a family is time-consuming, but what you're consumed with is up to you.

I advocate a date night, even if it's just once every few weeks. Get a babysitter while you have a quick dinner nearby. It's well worth it. When the kids were young, Mara and I were intentional about planning time together away from the kids. We both didn't want to look up one day and realize we'd gone five years without having a real conversation.

Asking for help requires planning. No one wants to be asked in the afternoon if they can babysit that evening, not even your parents. People who care about you will help you. In fact, they probably take great joy in doing so. This means if you don't ask them, you're stopping them from being fulfilled in that way.

WHEN YOU SAY YES TO ONE THING, YOU'RE SAYING NO TO SOMETHING ELSE

In the early days of Steiner Sports, I was grinding around the clock to build both a business and an industry. I said yes to everything whether I had the time, capacity, or money to make it happen. In the end, this strategy caused me a great deal of pain.

It took me a long time, but I finally came to grips with the fact that I couldn't say yes to everything. I stopped listening to what Little Brandon said I should and shouldn't do. I came to realize that feeling burned out because I'm stretched too thin is not a quality that extraordinary people possess. When I try to pull that 9,999-pound truck across the 10,000-pound capacity bridge, the only thing waiting for me on the other side is fear and disappointment. That's what happens when my to-dos don't get done.

I stopped going to every All-Star game, Super Bowl, trade

conference, and athlete appearance, and started making time for working out, having dinner at home with my family, resting, and other important things I'd neglected for far too long.

Yes, it's important to remain flexible and be open to helping people, but that flexibility must have limits. It's not good to be a doormat.

Some of us need to simplify our lives, to look at our daily routines and clear out the junk that drains us of both time and energy. Sometimes those drains come from things we were once excited about but have lost our passion for; at other times, they're things we've had thrust upon us and agreed to do because nobody else would. If something you do is important but you hate it, try to renegotiate a relationship with someone who can take it off your plate. If it's not important, stop doing it, and see if anyone notices. My guess is they won't.

ARE YOU THE HARDEST WORKING OR SMARTEST WORKING PERSON?

"If you're the smartest person in the room, you're in the wrong room."

—UNKNOWN

I learned that managing your time well isn't rocket science, but it does require effort and attention to keep from getting bogged down. A saying I live my life by is, "If it's not easy, it's not possible." I was guilty of making my daily agenda more difficult than it had to be, which made it impossible for me to succeed consistently and even more difficult to move toward becoming extraordinary. I was maxed on what I was doing and couldn't do more, which meant I couldn't be extraordinary.

That's why the MVP list and not-to-do list were game changers for me. I used the MVP list to keep my priorities where they should be. I created a not-to-do list and snatched the power back from those people and situations that were draining my energy and sucking up the resource I couldn't replenish—my time. I had to identify the assets in my life that could help me create a winnable game, then make them part of my team.

When I improved my relationship with time, focused on the important stuff, and removed the unimportant stuff, it opened up the door for extraordinary to come through and find me. I was wasting time on things that were insignificant, such as watching too many games, thinking about what I wanted for lunch or what I was going to wear, and doing meetings with people I didn't know just because they reached out. As a result, my priorities and the dreams I wanted to pursue were getting cast aside because I was bogged down in the busyness of everyday life. When I started managing my time effectively, it freed me up in more ways than I ever could have imagined.

CHAPTER 5

DREAM BIG, SAMPLE SMALL, FAIL FAST

"Why is a clever person wise? Because he knows what to do. Why is a stupid person foolish? Because he only thinks he knows."

—PROVERBS 14:8

During the process of resetting my life, I was searching for more clarity and more time to commit to my top priorities. As I examined how I spent my time at work, I found that I was SOS—stuck on stupid. I'd always prided myself on being resilient in the face of possible failure. I embodied all those messages we're bombarded with every day: *Don't quit! Fight through it! Keep going!* Don't get me wrong,

DREAM BIG, SAMPLE SMALL, FAIL FAST · 131

I'm a big fan of those qualities. The problem was that sometimes my ideas sucked, and I was too stubborn to realize it.

As I built my company, I fell into the trap of reading my own clippings. I started to think I could do anything I wanted, that every idea I had was a slam dunk. Due to my swelling ego and the fact I was SOS, right after I sold the company, I made more mistakes in one year than I had in my previous fourteen years in the industry combined.

Looking back at that mess, I saw I should have been a better quitter and let go of bad ideas. To help me move forward, I developed a three-step process to test if my ideas were worthwhile: dream big, sample small, fail fast. I like to say that losing gives you the blueprint for winning, and this blueprint has helped me and my team at Steiner Sports decide if we should stay with an idea or let it go.

Great ideas usually start with big dreams. When I dream big, I visualize a goal that I want to achieve. That's when the path to that achievement begins to take shape. I know the destination. How do I get there from where I am now?

Once I begin to pursue my goal with purpose and commitment, the extraordinary traits we talked about earlier—creativity, clarity, focus, determination, diligence, and thoughtfulness—initiated as a result of my efforts. Purpose is what lights the fire, but it's my big dreams that are the logs and the kindling that allow it to burn.

DREAMING IS FOR EVERYONE

"The dream is free. The hustle is sold separately."

—GEORGE "GK" KOUFALIS

I'm a big daydreamer and always have been. I need to picture my goal and fantasize about it before I can begin pursuing it with commitment. After selling the company, I saw that I needed to widen the dreams I was having. Up to that point, almost all of my dreams had been financial. I had to look inside my soul to find new dreams that related to my family and my health. I couldn't look online to find direction. It had to come from within.

Far too many people don't allow themselves time to daydream, or they ignore a dream when they have one. Some people I know think daydreaming is a young person's game. I hate that mindset because it puts up parameters where there shouldn't be any. When driving on a highway, you have to obey speed limits and laws. With dreaming, there are no speed limits or age limits. It's a free, unlimited resource.

I had to start dreaming like I was a teenager again, back

when I could imagine all the exciting possibilities. When you have a big dream, don't run from it. Instead, play it out and see where it takes you. I do this all the time. With certain dreams, I let them play out so much I'm ready to bring in producers and dramatize the whole thing!

I dreamt of starting a multimillion-dollar company well before Steiner Sports came into existence. By letting that dream play out, I saw the path that could lead me there.

I also like dreaming because it's low overhead and you can change it whenever you want. It's one of the few things you can completely control. It's your space, your thought, your dream, and nobody can jump into that unless you allow them.

DREAMING TO HELP OTHERS

Dreaming initiates purpose, which then ignites traits like creativity and focus. What you might not realize is that dreaming can also initiate empathy if you let it.

I don't just dream to help myself. I also dream to help others. When I dream big, I'm usually trying to solve a problem or accomplish a goal. I know these people around me have goals they'd like to achieve and problems they'd like to fix. Since dreaming is a free, unlimited resource, I like to spend some time dreaming on their behalf.

Before a sales call, I'll daydream where that client is right now and what their situation is like. I insert myself into that situation so I know what to say and how to act. I do the same thing when I call Mara or my kids. I picture where they are and what's going on with them.

This simple act fills me with empathy because I'm putting myself in someone else's shoes and imagining what their life is like. It goes back to forgetting yourself to fill yourself.

Are you taking full advantage of your capacity to dream? Daydreaming can be great from the standpoint of creativity and discovery, but it's also beneficial for your level of empathy, understanding, and compassion when you dream to help other people.

It's been an important aspect to my game in dealing with high-level athletes. When you put yourself in their shoes and imagine what it's like when people are coming at you from every direction, you start to understand their lives and feel compassion for them. When I start with that level of understanding, I'm able to serve them better as clients.

MOVE THE DREAM TOWARD A PURPOSE

"You didn't come this far only to come this far."

—UNKNOWN

A big dream has always been the initiator for me, a way to boost my confidence. At the same time, I know the dream can't be the dominator. A lot of stuff has to happen to make that dream a reality. I see my dreams as the start of a strategy, the first (and most important) step of which is to move that dream toward a purpose.

If I've got a big dream, I can start to connect to a purpose. Whether it's something cool with my family, like a vacation, serving a client, or providing a solution to a problem, I know I've got something special on my hands.

A dream isn't useful until you attach a purpose to it. One night, I was telling Crosby the story of the Mark Messier signed photo before bed. Funny enough, he fell asleep right at the beginning of the story, but I hung in there and kept telling it anyway. What I realized while telling the story was that everyone has one of those magical sports moments in their lives that they'll remember forever. We sold thousands of signed Messier photos because Rangers fans wanted to relive that moment every day. As I left Crosby's room, my wheels were already turning.

I went to my warehouse the next day and started going through the thousands of magazines I'd collected. I found hundreds of these iconic photos and realized that I could enrich people's lives by giving them a signed reminder of one of their favorite moments.

Now the purpose of my dream had grown to include serving others by giving them the chance to relive their magical sports moments. It was a complete differentiator for our company and the start of Steiner Collectibles (which would later become Steiner Sports). We weren't just selling autographs; we were selling moments. That was our tagline for the entire line of collectibles: "Remember the Moment."

To this day, people will come up to me and thank me for creating a piece of memorabilia that's enriched their lives. I cherish those interactions and consider what they say— the highest compliment a customer can give me.

You can accomplish anything when purpose is on your side. That said, it's important to know if the dream attached to that purpose is achievable.

To do that, you have to sample the dream to see if it's worth pursuing.

SAMPLE SMALL TO AVOID BIG LOSSES

"If you fall on your face, at least you're still moving forward."

Throughout my career, I've learned the hard way that just because you're aggressive and dream big doesn't mean you should go all out in pursuit of that dream. I wish I'd discovered a lot earlier in my career that it's smarter if you can sample small to see if your idea is actually as good as you think it is.

One product line we went all-in on was inexpensive, licensed collectibles like keychains and cardboard cut-outs of athletes. I wanted Steiner products to be in every Walmart and Kmart across the country. A lot of time, energy, and money went into developing these products. We were certain we had a great idea on our hands. Too bad we were dead wrong! The product line was a total failure. Our customers didn't like the products, and looking back, it didn't match what we were doing. The inventory also took up a ton of space in our warehouse, which I hadn't thought about. Had we sampled it before we launched, we could've seen that flop coming and saved a lot of time, frustration, and money.

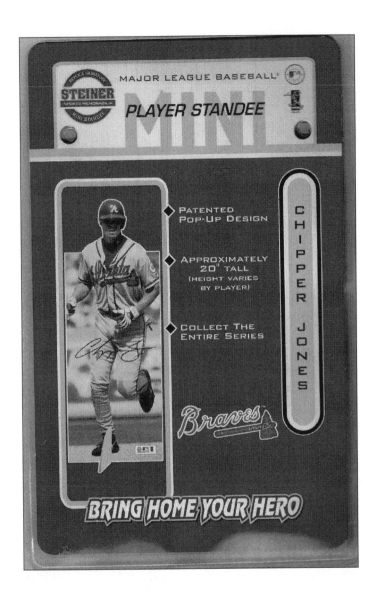

When we create a new product at Steiner Sports, we test it out before selling it to the general public. We'll mail the product to a small group of trusted customers and ask for their feedback. We're trying to get a sense of how our larger customer base might respond to this product. Is it worth selling, or should we walk away from it?

I believe resilience, diligence, and tenacity are important traits for entrepreneurs to have; however, I don't want you to confuse those qualities with stubbornness. I've watched people I know empty out their life savings and jeopardize their family's future just to see a bad idea through to the end. Here are three things I wish those entrepreneurs had understood before they pursued their idea:

- You need to understand your market and how your idea fits into it. Does your idea solve a problem?
- There's always risk involved. This is where most people get stuck.
- You need leadership because you've got to sell people on an idea they've never seen before and convince them that they need your solution.

The good news is that sampling small allows you to avoid some risk. If your idea looks like it's going to be successful, you can pursue it. If it looks like a failure, you can pull the rip cord early. Again, I'm not saying you should be a quitter. What I am saying is that some of the smartest businesspeople I know are some of the best quitters I've ever seen.

If you're just starting out and don't have a customer base to use for testing new ideas, run your idea by people you trust. Family members aren't always the best people to poll in these instances because typically they want to protect you from failure. Your loved ones don't want to see you get hurt, which is an admirable concern.

Eventually you'll need to get some analytics involved. The numbers don't lie, which means it's important to use them, even if you're not a numbers person. Analytics will help you see the full picture clearly. **Remember, you can't manage what you can't measure.**

Some people like to send out surveys and get good results that way. I hate surveys because I've found that people often don't know what they want until someone shows them they should want it. If you surveyed people in the early 1900s about developing a better method of transportation, they'd have asked for a faster horse and/or a more comfortable buggy.

It wasn't until Henry Ford showed Americans the automobile that their eyes were opened. Nobody knew what the hell a smartphone was, let alone wanted one, until Apple created the iPhone. People have limited imaginations, which in turn limits the usefulness of survey results. If you sample with a survey, I'd suggest using other tools, as well.

We send out a traffic light via email to our customers twice a year so they can express their level of satisfaction with our company. Here are their options:

- Red light: I'm unhappy.
- Yellow light: I'm happy, but I'd like someone to call me.
- Green light: I'm happy and everything is great.

STEINERSPORTS.COM™

Steiner Sports is 100% committed to ensuring that you are completely satisfied with the products you purchase, the events you attend and the service that we provide.

As we are always striving to improve your experience, we would love some feedback.

On the traffic light below, click on the corresponding colors for:

MAJOR ISSUE

SMALL ISSUE

ALL IS WELL

Red: Major issue that isn't currently resolved.

Yellow: Small issue (you've experienced technical difficulties that we weren't able to remedy for you)

Green: Good experience (satisfied with orders, customer service is good when there's been a problem, etc.)

Tell us because we want your experience with us to be the best it can possibly be.

Brandon Steiner

Whenever I try out a new idea, I find the person who does it the best and try to meet them. If I can't meet them, I use the internet to find out what it will take to beat the best.

I don't worry about hitting a home run when I sample my dream. I've never been a home run hitter. I always look to hit singles and see if my dream has enough traction for me to move forward. If my idea is a swing and a miss, I can go back to the dugout and regroup or keep hacking away, hoping to make contact. I know I always have a choice in how I handle the sample data and whether I move forward with my dreams.

IF YOU DON'T GO FOR YOUR GOALS, SOMEONE ELSE WILL USE YOU TO ACHIEVE THEIRS

When I sample my dream and it looks like it's going to succeed, my next step is to bring people alongside me who can help me realize that success. I can't always rely on myself to achieve my dreams. When I look at the most extraordinary people, I can see that their success is collaborative. They need people who can support and enhance their idea.

We saw it in the life of Steve Jobs. Whether you read the book or watched the movies, you probably remember the times he would tell people who worked with him they weren't good enough. Jobs was more of a jerk than you should be in these situations, but he was obsessed with finding the best people to help him achieve his dreams for Apple.

As we discussed in Chapter 2, talent acquisition is a manager's most important skill. Jobs understood this truth. He kept drilling down to find the right people. That's the best way to expedite your idea once you sample it and know it's got a chance at success.

FAILURE ISN'T THE OPPOSITE OF SUCCESS; IT'S A PART OF SUCCESS

"You don't make mistakes. Mistakes make you—smarter."

—HARRIET FROM THE MOVIE *THE LAST WORD*

One of the hardest things I've had to do was walk away from a dream I was passionate about. There are too many to list in this book, but one idea was a sports-themed ice cream chain called Last Licks. It was meant to be a sports bar for kids that would have TVs and collectibles all over the place, plus regular autograph sessions with players. We would have ice cream flavors named for famous athletes. "Licks" was an acronym that reflected our focus on kids: Learning—Interest—Creativity—Knowledge—Sportsmanship. My goal was to give kids a place they could call their own, the kind of place I never had growing up. A place where they could go after a Little League game or a hard day at school.

This idea came to me around the time I sold Steiner Sports to the Omnicom Group in 2002. I came home and told Crosby, who was nine at the time, that I'd sold the company and was buying the ice cream shop in town to turn it into a sports bar for kids. He wasn't thrilled with the idea, but once I told him ice cream was involved, that was all he needed to hear.

There's no such thing as an easy business, and this was no exception. In the end, we lost millions of dollars before we could sell off the stores. It was a solid idea, but our execution was terrible. We could never get the right managers in to run the stores, we made bad decisions on where to open stores, and we didn't know when to close stores.

I've never talked about this failure before, but it's probably the worst of my career. I learned a hard lesson: every failing business has a failing manager and/or owner.

Steiner Sports has landed some major partnerships in the past—the universities of Alabama and Syracuse, plus the Dodgers, Cubs, and Red Sox. I had big dreams for where those partnerships could go, but they didn't pan out in the end. With a big dream, there might come a point where the best idea is to give up and look for a new dream.

When I dig in and recklessly pursue a dream that's not achievable, it's usually a costly decision. It's been done before, but the underdog, rags-to-riches stories we all adore are the exceptions. History is littered with far more risk-takers who stubbornly pursued a dream only to see it fail. These folks ended up broke, burned out, or both.

I wish I'd been a better quitter many times throughout my career. Another of my big dreams was a product line where we took photos of great sports moments and let players tell their stories in their own words on the photos instead of just signing them. We had over 200 player stories, including Kirk Gibson's home run, Mariano's last game as a Yankee, Magic Johnson when he announced he had HIV, and Jim Craig winning the gold medal for USA Hockey in 1980. In my mind, it was the best idea since sliced bread.

Turns out I was wrong. The project flopped because customers didn't want a photo covered in words. Looking back, I was sprinting enthusiastically in the wrong direction with that idea. If I'd done a better job sampling that dream, I might've seen that failure coming.

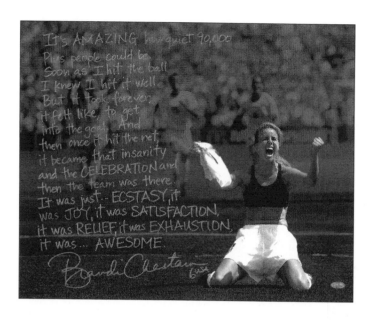

It's AMAZING how quiet 90,000 plus people could be. Soon as I hit the ball I knew I hit it well. But it took forever, it felt like, to get into the goal. And then once it hit the net, it became that insanity and the CELEBRATION and then the team was there. It was just... ECSTASY, it was JOY, it was SATISFACTION, it was RELIEF, it was EXHAUSTION, it was... AWESOME.

Brandi Chastain

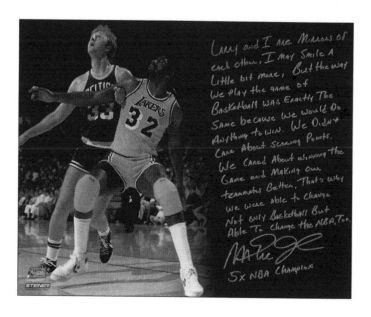

Larry and I are Mirrors of each other. I may Smile A Little bit more, But the way We play the game of Basketball was Exactly The Same because We would Do Anything to win. We Didn't Care About Scoring Points. We Cared About winning the Game and Making Our teammates Better. That's Why We were able to change Not only Basketball But Able To change the NBA, Too.

Magic Johnson
5x NBA Champion

I've stubbornly pursued dreams with new hires. I've brought in people with potential and spent months grooming them for a high-level position in our company. What I realized far too late with some of these hires was how bad the fit was from day one. No matter how much time and energy I poured into them, they'd never be an effective executive at Steiner Sports because they didn't match the culture we'd built.

Quitting does not equal failure. This is a tough pill for me to swallow because I'm competitive, and the losses sting too much. One of the reasons I'm no longer coaching basketball is that I can't stand losing. Even the best coaches lose a lot of games. If you're not equipped to handle the failure that comes with success, you won't last long in coaching. It's true, but you won't last long in business, either.

From 2006 to 2008, I was a volunteer assistant basketball coach under Coach Bill Murphy at New Rochelle High School, which was one of the top teams in the area. It was a dream for me to coach a top basketball team and see what that experience was like. Many days, I left the office at 3:00 to go to practice and work with the kids. I would ride the bus with them to games, spend hours in the film room, work out with the team at 6:00 a.m., and get water for the players during games.

In 2008, we had a team that, in my opinion, should've

won the state championship. We had three Division I players on that squad, but we lost our cool in the playoffs and got upset. It's a decade later, and I still have not recovered from that loss. However, I still have many great relationships with those kids to this day and cherish those years I got to spend coaching. It wasn't easy to do at forty-seven years old, but I had a dream of coaching basketball. Even though I found out that dream wasn't for me, I'm glad I got the chance to sample it.

If you want to increase how much you win, you've got to be prepared to handle more losing. When winning increases, your losing will increase too, and that's what broke me in many ways, and I wasn't prepared for it. I still struggle with losing and the toll it takes on me. I constantly have to remind myself that failure is part of winning; it's not the opposite of winning. The objective is not to avoid failure. The objective is to win more than you lose. If you go 51-49, you're still a winner. If you win more hands of blackjack than you lose in Vegas, you're probably coming home with some dough. My problem is that I hate losing more than I love winning.

Sometimes I've lost when I dreamed big, but I always learned something valuable from the experience. Coaching basketball was like that. Knowledge is power because I can't buy it or trade for it. I've got to earn it. Sometimes knowledge is earned the hard way, but I won't soon forget what I learned. When I reframe a loss as the opportunity to gain insight, it keeps my mind focused on the positives instead of succumbing to disappointment and fear.

Don't let your ego get in the way either. To quote Ryan Holiday, "Ego is the enemy." When our dreams are entirely self-centered, we focus on the money and fame our ideas can bring rather than how our idea can help others. When our ego steers the ship, we can pursue a dream further than it's worth because we're obsessed with earning the rewards.

You've got to have a little ego—MLB players couldn't get in front of 50,000 people and hit a 100-mile-per-hour fastball without it—but you can't let it get to a point where things don't make sense. You've got to keep your ego in check. You also have to be careful not to let your ego get so bruised by failure that you don't get back up to the plate after a strikeout. The Last Licks failure left me numb for a couple years, and I regret not picking myself up sooner.

I learned that sometimes my dreams just suck, and that's OK. Maybe they were good at the time, but now they don't work like I'd hoped. I look at the situation as an opportunity to learn and grow, cut my losses, and move on. If I've still got purpose, I'll find a new dream.

CHAPTER 6

YOUR CHILDREN'S SUCCESS IS A BIG PART OF YOUR SUCCESS

"I'm not a parenting expert. In fact, I'm not sure that I even believe in the idea of 'parenting experts.' I'm an engaged, imperfect parent and a passionate researcher. I'm an experienced mapmaker and a stumbling traveler. Like many of you, parenting is by far my boldest and most daring adventure."

—BRENÉ BROWN

One night my wife came to bed frustrated. She was struggling to get our daughter, Nicole, out of bed in the morning. I couldn't believe waking our daughter up could be that difficult, so I offered to get her up the next morning. Mara happily handed off the responsibility.

I walked down to Nicole's room and told her the plan. If she brushed her teeth, got dressed, gathered all her school supplies, and was downstairs at 8:05 eating breakfast and ready to leave by 8:15, I'd give her $5 to spend on whatever she wanted. The next morning, she was ready to walk out the door by 8:10. It was a miracle!

I thanked her and gave her the promised financial reward.

She said, "Dad, I've gotta tell you, this is the easiest $5 I've ever made."

I responded, "Me too—I bet your mom $10 that I'd have you downstairs, ready to go, by 8:15!"

I love that story because it illustrates the importance of having fun with your kids and why you shouldn't get stuck in the way you were parented. Each relationship between a parent and a child is unique, which means as parents, we have to stay flexible. My mother never offered me $5 to get out of bed, but that doesn't mean I can't do it with my kids.

I know parenting is a sensitive subject. I debated even including a chapter in this book about it. Ultimately, I knew I couldn't tell you my story without sharing the changes I've made in how I parent my kids and the difference it's made in their lives and in mine.

My goal with this chapter is not to tell you how to parent but to share some of what I've learned about trying to be the best parent I can be. I knew that having some financial success and not having parented to the best of my ability would have been a complete failure for me, so I try to learn everything I can about successful parenting.

If you question people as to why they work hard to earn a living, most will tell you they do it for their family. Yet to look at the daily lives of these same people, often their kids get the short end of the stick on the other pillars of success and happiness.

The sentiment you've seen throughout this book continues here. As a parent, I've learned it's not enough to say something is a priority. Your actions have to back up what you say; otherwise, your kids just aren't going to believe you.

I've worked with some really difficult people in some hard jobs, but I've come to realize that **parenting is the hardest job in the world**. It's also the most important job because it has a profound impact on the lives of the people closest to you. Regardless of your financial standing, career success, or good health, if your kids are miserable, you're miserable.

As a parent, you're only as happy as your most unhappy kid.

YOU CAN PARENT YOUR KIDS TO SUCCESS

My kids are my top priority, so they get my best time and energy. I pay as much attention to my children as I do my bank account. After years of focusing on making money, what I learned the hard way is that I don't need a lot of money to be a good parent. I just need to be present with my kids and let them know they're important to me.

When Crosby was sixteen, I was having dinner with him and a couple of my friends. We were going to a Billy Joel concert and had stopped to eat beforehand.

As we ate, one of my friends asked Crosby an interesting question.

"Do you realize how lucky you are to be Brandon Steiner's son?" he asked. "You attend amazing events, sit in great seats, meet celebrities and players, and live in a big house."

I was caught off guard, curious to see how my son would respond.

"Don't get me wrong, I'm grateful for the life my dad has provided me," he replied. "But that doesn't mean I have it any easier than other kids. We all face stress and pressure to do well in school, regardless of our financial situation or what our parents provide. Do you know how hard it is to grow up in Scarsdale, where every kid has a BMW? Where every kid has a tutor for every subject because they all want to go to Harvard? The competition is crazy."

I had never thought about it that way before. You think that because you're in one of the better neighborhoods and your kids are attending a good school that they bypass the difficulties of growing up, but they don't. Unfortunately, a lot of parents operate with this assumption. Their kids didn't ask for the "good life," and just because they have it doesn't mean they're immune to peer pressure and the weight of expectations. As a parent, I needed to realize that regardless of what neighborhood I was raising my kids in, regardless of the wealth we had, it's a tremendous challenge for a kid to grow up in this day and age.

I realized that the standard of living I provided for my kids is important, but it's far more important that I be there and help them build a successful life. That's one of the reasons I sold my company. I was MIA more than I would've liked in the lives of my kids, and that absence was putting a strain on our entire family. My focus had to change. My priorities had to be rearranged.

Making your kids a top priority can help you parent them to success. Keep in mind, though, that your version of success may not match their version. Every parent has dreams for their children and visualizes what an ideal life looks like for them. We get in trouble when we stick to our ideas instead of seeing who our children are and following their lead.

A valuable lesson I learned is you can parent your kids to success, but you can't dictate their success. Good parents adapt based on their kid's strengths, weaknesses, imperfections, and quirks.

I've had friends whose kids weren't big sports fans. You could see the disappointment in their eyes when they talked about it. What they were failing to realize is that just because your kids aren't into what you're into doesn't make them anything less than spectacular kids. Find out what they're spectacular at and enjoy that with them.

"The privilege of a lifetime is being who you are."
—JOSEPH CAMPBELL

My mother was very paranoid because both of my brothers wanted to go into theater, dancing, and acting. We had so little money, and it's difficult to get into those industries. She pushed hard for them not to pursue those interests, but because I was interested in business, she showed me support. I appreciated her love at the time, but looking back, that wasn't fair to my brothers. My mom should've encouraged them to chase that dream. Even if they failed, the journey would've been worth the effort. I'm not sure my brothers got a chance to do what they were gifted to do, which is a crime.

You've got to be all-in when your kids work hard to be successful at something. If you give lackluster support, kids pick up on that and can get discouraged. As our kids have gotten older, mine and Mara's main jobs now are being consultants, helping our kids when they seek our advice and being cheerleaders for whatever they're trying to do.

FEWER RULES CAN LEAD TO BETTER RESULTS

"I had one rule at Indiana: don't do anything to piss me off."
—BOB KNIGHT

In my house growing up, we had zero rules. Crazy, right? So in parenting, I always felt there was no need to have a hundred rules because what would happen is I'd have one or two rules that made sense, then add ninety-eight more to get to a hundred. I always favored simplicity when it came to rules and expectations for my kids (and employees too). When you focus on the important stuff, kids tend to remember what's expected of them.

I had only three rules for my kids:

1. 1. Be a good sister, brother, son, or daughter.
2. 2. Treat others with kindness and be a good friend.
3. 3. You don't have to be the best in school. Just do your best.

I never wanted my rules to feel burdensome to my kids. I figured if they focused on being kind people who tried hard in school, the rest would take care of itself.

My three kids are still a work in progress, but I see glimpses every now and then that reaffirm the importance of focusing on who your kids really are, not who you're hoping they'll be.

I see parents chasing their kids and yelling at them over every little thing, and it makes me shake my head. I think micromanagement can drive kids crazy. Do you really want to argue about your kid's bedtime or whether or not their room is clean? Or do you think it might be useful to ask your kids when they want to go to bed or whether they think it's good to live in a filthy, messy room?

What I have learned and have to remind myself is to save the discipline for the important stuff. That way, when I need to use discipline, my kids know I mean business.

It's not watered down by all the other times I've lost my mind on my kids for breaking one of my hundred rules.

YOU HAVE TO TRUST YOUR CHILDREN

"The best proof of life is trust."

—JOYCE BROTHERS

We often parent based on the way we were parented, but respect, simplicity, and trust should be our top priorities. If you know you've raised your kids right, trust them to make good decisions.

I was reminded of that principle by Elwood Pennington, the father of former Jets quarterback Chad Pennington. Elwood, Chad, and I had planned a Sandlot Wisdom Q&A session for parents and kids at the Emelin Theatre in Mamaroneck. The goal was to show the dynamic between parents and their kids when their kids are playing sports. I wish I had stayed with this idea. There are a lot of parents who need guidance on how to handle their kids when they're playing organized sports. That's what Elwood and Chad were there to discuss with the audience. The day of the event, I arrived late. When Elwood asked what happened, I told him I'd been dealing with a situation involving my daughter, Nicole. She wanted to ride her bike across a heavily trafficked street, and rather than letting her do that, I told her she should wait until her mother got home so she could discuss it with her.

Having a good relationship with both men, Elwood was quick to point out the problem with my response. Despite saying that I trusted my daughter, my reply said I didn't trust her decision-making. Instead of telling her to wait for her mother, I should've asked Nicole her opinion on the dangers of a nine-year-old biking across that busy road and if she thought that was a good idea. Could she find an alternate route? Did she feel OK about crossing a busy street on her bike? Then, after weighing the pros and cons, if she still wanted to bike that road, I should've let her do that (unless I thought she'd be in serious danger).

Elwood helped me see that I needed to ask my kids what they thought and let them make their own decisions as often as possible. I had to remember that kids have egos too. One line Crosby likes to use when we're arguing or I'm trying to discipline him is, "Dad, I'm a person too, you know." (I wish I had a tape of my son, a ten-year-old, hitting me with that line.) So when Nicole asked me if she could do that, I should have asked her, "At nine years old, how do you think it will be crossing such a busy street?"

That's a tough pill to swallow as a parent, isn't it? I know I've struggled with giving my kids more independence and relinquishing my role in their decision-making. Mara and I believe the earlier we give our kids the opportunity to make decisions and think for themselves, the earlier they will learn the vital concepts of repercussions and responsibility.

Mara and I felt we could start with little decisions, such as ordering in restaurants. Most kids don't get to choose what they want because their parents order for them. My mother never let me order anything. I still have trouble ordering in restaurants to this day. In clothing stores, parents decide what their kids should wear instead of letting them pick some outfits. Some kids may not care what they eat or wear, but if your child does have ideas, I'd encourage you to let them make decisions based on those thoughts. Doing so gives them confidence in their decision-making and lets everyone evaluate the effects of those choices.

We always took a vote on where to go for vacation. Crosby, Nicole, and Keith always knew their voice mattered in our house. Their opinion had value. Sometimes the vacation wasn't what they expected, like when we ended up in Dubai because Crosby saw an indoor ski slope in the middle of the desert, and it was his turn to pick the vacation. My kids took charge of some aspects of the planning; if something went wrong, they learned to take responsibility. Sometimes you have to play things out with your kids and not be afraid to let them fail or get into difficult situations and realize they didn't think things through.

One night, Nicole stayed up late to watch a TV show she liked. I reminded her she had a test the next day, but she insisted she felt fine. I asked her the next day how she did on the test, and her response was, "Not so great." Sure enough, she was so exhausted that she bombed the test. She knew she should've gotten more sleep. I could've forced her to go to bed earlier, but I let her learn in a way that would stick with her. Failure can provide the best opportunities for learning no matter what your age.

YOU CAN NEGOTIATE WITH YOUR KIDS

When it comes to bargaining, some parents handle their kids like the US government handles terrorists: we do not negotiate! I'm just the opposite. Everything is negotiable with my kids. As you saw with the story about Nicole, if I want them to do something, I'll offer them something they want in return. Isn't that what we do as adults? If we work forty hours a week, we'll get a paycheck. If we eat right and exercise, we'll lose weight. If we save money, we'll get to retire and live out our later years sipping beer on the beach.

As parents, we all want our children to do the right thing because they know it's the right thing to do, but it doesn't always work that way. Sometimes, just like with adults, a little ethical bribe is needed to get kids moving in the right direction.

I did this with Keith, who was part of a program called Scarsdale STEP, where the community rallies behind one kid each year to help them get to college and give them opportunities they would not have gotten otherwise. These kids come from different parts of the country and usually a disadvantaged situation. The program is supposed to last two years for each kid, but Keith has been part of our family for almost a decade now.

Keith came to live with us at sixteen years old from South Dakota, where he'd lived on an Indian reservation. When he showed up to our house, he had all his possessions in a shopping bag. He was behind in school, so Mara and I made it our goal to get him ready for college. We got him the best tutors, and he started making great progress in all his classes.

During this time, Keith also tried out for the football team. Two months into playing football, he made an announcement one morning during breakfast. Keith wouldn't be attending any more tutoring sessions. All he wanted to do was play in the NFL. He thought this would be a way for him to provide for his family. He had a *why*, and I give him credit for that, but we had to remind him that the number of kids who make it to Division I, let alone to the NFL, is a very small percentage.

I looked over at Mara and thought she was about to have

a heart attack. To diffuse the situation, I took Keith out for a drive. After a few minutes, I pulled over to the side of the road, killed the engine, and looked Keith square in the eyes.

"We took you in and made you part of this family to help you get right academically and socially," I told him. "We want you to get into the best schools and do amazing things with your life. You can't do that or go to the NFL without good grades, so I'll make you a deal. I'll get you the best equipment, a personal trainer, and bring some NFL players by the house to show you how to play the game. But if you miss one tutoring session, you get nothing."

Keith never missed another tutoring session. He also took advantage of what I offered him—a trainer, cool equipment, and meeting players. He got hurt playing football his senior year, sidetracking his NFL dreams, but the tutoring continued, and Keith excelled in school. He received the prestigious Gates Scholarship and graduated from Villanova University. He was also awarded the Truman Scholarship, meaning he can attend grad school pretty much wherever he wants.

Before we took that drive, I understood what was important to Keith and used it to get the behavior Mara and I knew would benefit his future, even if he didn't realize it.

It's not just the small stuff you can negotiate with your kids. The bigger the stakes are, however, the more you have to understand and respect what it is your kids truly want.

YOUR ATTITUDE DETERMINES YOUR ALTITUDE

When your kid's behavior is not right, don't kill the kid. Kill the behavior.

We caught Nicole drinking underage with some friends, which happens with a lot of kids. Nicole was a great kid who did well in school and was very creative, but when we caught her drinking, we took away her computer, car, phone, and didn't let her go out on weekends. She thought we were being too tough on her. I explained that she was still a rock star to us, but her behavior wasn't acceptable. We were killing the behavior itself, not her as a person or as our daughter. When your kids break your rules or break the law, what are the repercussions going to be? Are you, your spouse, or coparent on the same page when it comes to enforcing those repercussions?

One thing I learned was to never reprimand my kids in public, even when they're acting like an ass or being unruly. All that does is embarrass them and cause them to act out more. Remember, your kid has an ego, same as you. Don't bruise that ego in front of their friends. Instead, pull them aside and give them a chance to regroup. When you do, your chances of regaining order go up significantly.

Giving your kid feedback should not be much different than giving an employee review. Ask them to amplify good behaviors and reduce bad behaviors. Let them know when they're on track and do so often. We as parents assume our kids know how we feel, but I've found that constant feedback is helpful when it's constructive and leads with the positives.

Parents frequently ask me how they can avoid having their kid feel entitled, especially when the parents are doing well. Here's why I appreciate that question. **Just because a kid was born on third base doesn't mean he hit a triple.** But if you let him think that as he grows up, he'll spend his life believing the world owes him whatever he wants.

The first step I took to avoid entitlement was being honest about what I had instead of pretending I didn't have it. I didn't shy away from my success just to keep my children's feet on the ground. I also showed them how I achieved success so they would understand it didn't just land on my lap. I took them to work as often as I could in order to show them the good, the bad, and the ugly of what it takes to support the life we all enjoyed.

I made sure they understood that I'd earned the beautiful house, luxury cars, and expensive vacations, and that I was choosing to share it with them. When they got older, they could decide to share what they earned with their children.

I try to teach my kids that the highest level of success isn't about what you have but what you can give back to others. I want my children to understand from the time they're young that the real gift is how they can affect other people's lives in a positive way. **All the things they have are just things.**

We always tried to show Crosby, Nicole, and Keith the importance of charity and the joy we got from serving my community. As parents, Mara and I got to serve as our kids' GPS in that way, showing them the true paths to success and happiness. We wanted to instill within our kids a selfless desire to serve others, not a selfish desire to serve themselves.

BE THERE FOR YOUR KIDS EARLY AND OFTEN

If your kids commit to something, they should stick with it, even if it's not convenient. Sometimes we inadvertently signal to our kids that's it's OK to not fulfill a promise or not keep your word. If you let your kids make their own decisions, they must stick by that decision. Parents make the mistake of letting their kids off the hook. They want it to be easy for them, but life's not easy. You're setting your kids up to struggle later on.

This was not an easy process for me. It's tough to sit back and not give my kids the right answer, knowing full well it might cause them to fail. As a parent, I don't help my kids if I fight their battles for them. I had to teach them to fight for themselves.

When I was talking to Jay Wright, head coach at Villanova, one of the things he told me was, "It's easy to play in a game in which everything goes well. We don't have a lot of signs at the gym, but the sign we do have says that **we practice difficult situations so that when we get in difficult situations, our kids are prepared to deal with them.**"

This was a great lesson I learned with my kids. Mara and I talked with them about the tough subjects like sex and drugs so they'd be prepared to handle those situations.

I want my kids to do the right thing and not look for short-cuts, which starts with thinking about the right thing. I tell my kids that if they think about the wrong thing, it doesn't stay hidden in their minds. That kind of thinking will come out in their actions at some point.

Take time for these important lessons when your kids are

younger. When you give advice to your kids at five years old, you still have a chance to shape them as they grow. The younger you can have these conversations and transfer these messages, the better. My mother always told me I should talk to my kids the minute I brought them home from the hospital, so that's what I did. You may think you have plenty of time when your kids are young, but I learned it goes by a lot faster than you think.

When your kids get to high school, you probably won't have as much interaction with them. At that age, they're in clubs and hanging out with friends. It's still important for you to be around at that point, even though you are not interacting with each other as much. Think of it like you're the boss of a company: even though your employees may not come into your office, they know you're there. Your kids need to know you're available when they need you. Your presence is just as important as it ever was.

Assuming you maintain strong relationships with your children, you'll actually have more conversations with them as they move into adulthood. Like many parents, I went through the phase where I was the stupid parent. Because I made an effort to talk to my kids when they were younger, my kids realized when they moved into adulthood that I actually wasn't stupid but somewhat smart, and they started asking me for advice again.

I saw that I could forge strong bonds with my children through my words and actions. When my kids walk into a room, I want them to see my face light up. My reaction to seeing my kids shows them they're important. Every night when I would put them to sleep, I would tell them how important they are and that I'm there to protect them. I also told them they had the stuff inside them to be great one day. Kids want to feel loved and protected.

OFFER YOUR KIDS PASSIONATE SUPPORT

One of the things I had to stop doing when I was home was getting excited only when I thought about my business. Instead, I got excited about what my kids were passionate about. I think it's important to follow your kid's passion, not yours. You can groom your child for the Ivy League or the New York Yankees, but only if that's their passion. The road kids are on is not always an obvious one. As with all things in life, stay flexible. Having preconceived notions of what you want your kids to be can lead to disappointment.

I got into what my kids were into because I wanted to support them in that way. It was another measure of giving my kids the confidence that they can make good decisions, especially when it's a minor thing and not a life-or-death decision.

Crosby went through a phase when he was younger where

he only wore red. Instead of telling him to wear other colors or that he looked like a red-hot chili pepper, we went shopping and bought him more red clothing. For three years, he wore red socks, sweatpants, and shirts. A lot of parents would be worried about things like that, but there's nothing wrong with supporting a kid who loves red.

Later, Crosby developed a love for trains, so we got crazy into trains. We went to the train museum almost every week and visited other train museums around the US. We brought in a designer to build a whole train station in his room. Everywhere we went, I tried to take the train, even if it was a long distance. A lot of times, we passed our destination because Crosby didn't want to get off the train.

Nicole loved these beautiful glass fish when she was younger, so we helped her collect them. She also loved pink and purple, so, as much as possible, we made everything pink and purple. For a while, Nicole only ate pasta with a little butter on it. It was not exciting going out to eat with her, but rather than force her to eat other things, we went with it, knowing at some point she'd crave more variety.

As a quirky kid myself (some would say I was weird or there was something wrong with me), I know kids can get quirky about things the same way adults do. I didn't bring conflict to these minor issues, choosing to focus on the important stuff. I enjoyed the imperfections because I knew they made my kids who they are.

I try to support my kids as they explore new interests. It's OK if that interest doesn't match the perfect vision I'd built up for them in my head. Our interests grow and evolve as we get older. I now know that just because my kid was into dance or soccer when they were younger didn't mean they'd discovered their life's great purpose. They're still exploring to discover who they are and what they love. I want to join them on that journey!

As parents, we get joy from watching our children do something they love doing. That same feeling you get when you're pursuing a purpose with commitment and the passion is flowing is amplified when it comes to your kids. I promise that you won't care if it's what you envisioned them doing from the time they were babies. Go with the flow and support your child's pursuits. You have no idea how much it will mean to them.

Having grown up in a dysfunctional family, I know how devastating it can be to not have unconditional support from your parents in all aspects of life—physical, mental, and emotional. I'm sure there are a lot of you out there who can relate.

When you're young, you can't articulate how much it means to live with a sense of safety and security. It's not until you're older that you see the effects of your parents' support, how their guiding hand kept you from feeling empty and vulnerable. If you grew up without that support like I did, you want the exact opposite for your own children.

"We live in a world in which we need to share responsibility. It's easy to say, 'It's not my child, not my community, not my world, not my problem.' Then, there are those who see the need and respond. I consider those people my heroes."

—FRED ROGERS

Of all the purposes I've had in my life, none has been more important than building a thriving marriage and raising successful, happy children. Family means everything to me, which is why I moved to make sure my wife and kids get my best energy and full attention most days. To me, there's no greater fortune worth seeking. No financial legacy can compare to the legacy of your children. They're the ultimate testament to what kind of person you were. It took me a while to realize this, and it saddens me to know there were times when my children didn't get my best energy.

PART III

FITNESS

CHAPTER 7

THE NEGATIVE ENERGY TRAP

"Some of us think holding on makes us strong. But sometimes it is letting it go."

—HERMANN HESSE

Faith, fortune, and fitness don't exist independent of each other in your life. I realized they're all tied in together, pushing me closer to extraordinary achievement.

I can't believe how many mornings I woke up not feeling the best or struggling to find enough energy to make it through the day. Poor nutrition and a lack of exercise were to blame, but I also discovered I was stuck in a negative energy trap.

A negative energy trap is often rooted in fear and disappointment. I had all these negative experiences and emotions floating around inside me, clogging me up so I couldn't create purposeful energy. I hadn't come clean with stuff from my childhood that was affecting my ability to fully embrace fitness: a mom who weighed over 400 pounds, a home that lacked healthy food, and the fact we never talked about eating right or getting exercise.

I had to shake loose of the mediocre tendencies these feelings had created. I had to give myself permission to be as healthy as I could possibly be, which was a big shift for me. Part of that meant going to sleep earlier and waking up earlier, going in to work later so I could work out in the morning, leaving work on time Wednesday nights to play basketball at my house, and saying no to meetings or events that would pull me away from the time each week where I focus on my fitness.

It wasn't easy to make these changes because negative energy is nasty. It didn't sit quietly inside of me, and since I'd let it fester, it had become strong and loud. I'm glad I dealt with it when I did, because letting negative energy fester too long can lead to serious mental health issues like anxiety, addiction, depression, or suicidal thoughts.

I learned that before you look at diet or exercise as the reason your energy is lacking, you have to take a look inside and see if there's some negative energy you need to come clean with first. **Don't just focus on what you're eating. Focus on what's eating you.**

As I built Steiner Sports, I was climbing a ladder, but it wasn't on solid ground. The higher I climbed, the more unsafe I felt. I knew I needed to make serious changes because when I looked in the mirror, I didn't like the person I saw staring back. I couldn't believe how little I knew about my most important asset: my body. I knew the exact numbers in my bank account and was doing well financially, but I was a wreck physically—burned out, overweight, and struggling to create energy for each day.

If you had one car when you got your driver's license that you had to keep for the rest of your life, wouldn't you take excellent care of that car? Of course! You'd get the oil changed, keep the tires aired up, and wash and wax that baby regularly.

Shouldn't we treat our bodies the same way? We only get one for our entire life, and unlike a car, we can't go to the dealership and swap it out for a new model after a few years.

Before I started thinking that way, I was working out a little bit and eating all right from time to time, but I realized I needed to do more after a Navy SEAL came to my office to give a talk to my employees. He helped me see that what I was doing was not enough and that I needed to dig deeper. My problem was I lacked focus. I decided to dig into health, diet, and fitness the same way I'd built Steiner Sports—brick by brick.

But first, I had to deal with my negative energy trap. I had to ask myself why the hell I preferred to stay at work instead of coming home to see my family. I was married to an amazing woman I adored, had kids I loved spending time with, and lived in a gorgeous house. It was insane that I was avoiding going home to that.

Looking inside, again I found a lot of negative energy from my childhood. As a kid, my home was cold and empty. We had no food in the fridge. Work was an escape for me. I worked long hours to avoid coming home to a place that I found dark and depressing. I'd let that mind-set continue unchecked into my adult life despite it not being true anymore.

I also discovered some false beliefs about my self-worth. You see, coming from a broken home, I had long carried with me the weight and the guilt of dysfunction. That guilt often kept me from feeling valuable as a human being, so I tied my self-worth into my net worth. That meant when I did well at work, I felt great. But failure caused my self-worth to plummet. I also overemphasized work in my personal relationships and conversations. What I figured out was that my self-worth and my net worth have nothing to do with each other. **I'm a valuable person regardless of how much money I make.** All those years I'd been tying them together, I'd been making a big mistake.

It took me a long time, but I finally accepted that I'm a valuable person regardless of whether I'm winning at work or not. Once I started doing that, the negative energy trap became unclogged inside me, and I focused on improving my sleep, diet, and exercise.

Now I'm capable of producing purposeful energy, which has allowed me to move from doing well to achieving extraordinary things in different areas. But I had to do the dirty work of digging into my negative energy trap and handling those feelings in a healthy way.

It wasn't easy, and it's something I'm still working on, but the effort is totally worth it. I appreciate the fact I have an amazing therapist who worked hard with me to get through some of this, which was very painful and difficult for me.

You've got to take responsibility for the energy you bring into a room and into your everyday life. I've seen it happen often that people will accuse in order to excuse.

They'll blame their boss for overworking them or the fact they have kids at home for why their energy levels are low. I've learned you can't blame others for your problems. You also have to plan ahead and forecast for your health as you age and changes begin occurring rapidly. If you continue the same behaviors throughout your life and expect the same level of health, you're in for a world of surprises and those surprises aren't really good ones.

The body keeps score, and it always wins. I wish I was reading this book at twenty so I could have prepared myself. **We've all heard the saying, "Don't dress for the job you have; dress for the job you want." In the same way, don't prepare for the health you have but for the health you want.** If you're young and your health is good, it'll require work to keep it that way.

PLAN TOMORROW'S HEALTH TODAY

When I was a kid in Brooklyn, my health was planned for me between activities, sports, and play dates. I was always on the move, going to the park or schoolyard to play handball, box ball, stickball, touch football, street hockey, capture the flag—all types of games, all day, every day. In college, I was running all over the place, staying active every day by staying involved. The change came when I shifted into my career and began to slow down. I was traveling more, spending more time at a desk, and didn't move around as much. I used to be moving several hours a day, now I was moving a few minutes a day.

As an adult, no one was scheduling a play date or planning my health for me. I had to do it myself because my body was changing as I got older. I could no longer digest what I used to eat in college.

I see a lot of people now in their forties and fifties who aren't as effective, not due to declining abilities but because they don't feel well. They're not making the adjustments necessary nutritionally, stretching, exercise, and sleep. In my experience, it's not enough to know how these factors impacted my health. I had to schedule the necessary changes by blocking off time for me. I had to remind myself that my body was my biggest asset and that I wanted it to be around for as long as possible. Rather than being the richest man of all time, the question I now raised was, could I set the record for being the healthiest man who lived the longest of all time?

I know 100 percent for sure that if I hadn't made those adjustments in my forties and fifties, I might not be here right now. I have every intention of living a full life, which is, according to today's numbers, somewhere in your eighties. If I had kept going along the same path, I maybe would've made it to halftime, but I would've been spending a lot of time in doctor's offices, in one hospital after another, and taking a ton of pills just to maintain my unhealthy feeling. When it comes to my fitness, that's my purpose: I don't want to spend the next few decades in hospital rooms and doctor's offices. I'm afraid of hospitals and doctor's offices. I think it goes back to watching my mom constantly taking pills and staying in hospital rooms because her health was so poor. Honestly, it scared the shit out of me. That purpose alone has given me the strength to make sure I stay on a healthy trail.

To achieve that purpose, I had to forecast what I needed and then commit to making it happen every day. **My "some days" had to become my "every days" when it came to health and fitness.** It included making simple changes, like buying the right kinds of foods. I had to stop doing dumb things with my nutrition, like eating a full bowl of cereal after I worked out or snacking on unhealthy foods all day at the office. I thought I was making a healthy choice with those behaviors, but in reality, I was loading up on calories. I also committed financially to this effort by turning a room in our house into a gym.

I've always felt I needed a reason to make changes and increase my energy level. I've shared mine with you. Maybe yours is that you want to accomplish more in a day, or you realize you don't have sufficient energy when you arrive home to be a good spouse or parent. Creating purposeful energy means coming up with a purpose for being healthier. It's tempting to think of purpose as some grand, overarching vision, but you can have a lot of little purposes that, when taken together, are as important as one big purpose.

YOU'VE GOT TO FIND YOUR HAPPY DAYS!

One exercise that was really helpful for me was asking myself, what were my happiest days? What made those days so wonderful? As I went through this exercise, I was shocked and disappointed by how little effort I'd put into replicating those happy days. I committed to having more happy days so I could feel that happy again more often—playing pickup basketball in the park, visiting my favorite Turkish bathhouse for a steam, and more vacations with my family.

People often say they'll enjoy happy days after their family gets situated or they've saved up money. You want to avoid that mindset because your tomorrows aren't guaranteed. Rather than waiting, mix some of what makes you happy into each day or each week.

Here's an example: I love black-and-white cookies. We had very little money when I was a kid, but any time I could scrounge together fifteen cents, I tried to buy myself one of those cookies. As a kid, eating a black-and-white cookie constituted a happy day. Nowadays, I can eat those cookies whenever I want. I don't, obviously, because I'd weigh 300 pounds if I did, but I'll strategically work a black-and-white cookie into my diet some weeks.

Sometimes what makes us happy is materialistic. That's OK! My daughter says I have enough workout clothes and I don't need any more. She's not wrong, but I like wearing new stuff. It's fun, and it motivates me to work out on days I feel like staying in bed.

Happy days gave me purposeful energy and have transformed the stuff I dreaded doing into the stuff I looked forward to doing, like working out. I used to be one of those people who didn't enjoy exercising. If you're one of those people, do what I did: put a nice TV in your home gym, create a killer playlist, and invest in some nice headphones. When I did that, I started waking up every morning excited to work out because I'd made it fun.

If you dread going to the office each day, make your workspace fun. Sometimes I go into someone's office, and there's not a thing on the walls or the shelves. There are no family photos or photos from vacations. The furniture is all beat up, and I wonder how happy this person could be in this environment. Why wouldn't they have some of their favorite pictures up, a nice desk, and a comfortable chair?

To put it simply: make the most important thing your favorite thing.

When that transformation happens, what you once dreaded becomes one of your favorite parts of the day. A black hole on your schedule is suddenly a rainbow. It's the most liberating feeling in the world and a great way to use your purposeful energy, but to get to that rainbow, you've got to deal with the rain.

HOW I START MY DAY

No matter what I have going on, I know every day can potentially be a happy day. The first part of a happy day is starting off with gratitude. When I wake up each morning, I'm grateful for the day I have in front of me and the people I have in my life. I focus on the most positive stuff I have in my day and try to transform what's negative into something positive. Once I'm filled with gratitude, I take time to think rather than jumping into my routine. I use the first thirty minutes of each day to ponder. The hardest work we do is thinking, so I figure why not do it first thing in the morning when I'm fresh?

Each day is a blank sheet of paper. How will you fill it? Sometimes I fill it with dreams. These can be dreams for myself, my company, or other people. How can I make someone's day better or help another person accomplish something that's important to them?

One of my favorite things to do when I'm a little off track is go up to Syracuse and work out in the Melo Center with their coaches and trainers or talk to students at Falk College. We all need a place where we can escape from time to time and reset things. Syracuse is that place for me. When I'm working out with the top athletes on campus, their energy seeps into me. Visiting with the students reminds me to get myself into a learning mode.

Other times, I'll fill that page with notes to follow up with people. I'll review conversations I've had and think about the response I want to give. I always try to respond rather than react, but to do that means taking time during my day to think about my response.

The second part of a happy day comes from recognizing when you're having one. I was very quick to recognize my bad days and let the world know about them, but how often did I let the world know I was having a happy day? How often was I showing gratitude for the people who made that day happy? Some days are so good I don't want them to end. I always try to recognize those days when I'm on a roll at work. I may get home late, but I want to hang on to that day for as long as I can.

I try to recognize those happy days and appreciate them but also take note of what makes them happy. I know what made me happy in the past, but it's also crucial to know when something new brings joy to my day. It could be meeting someone new, enjoying a great lunch, or helping someone in a new way. I make note of these happy moments.

Energy and efficiency help me have more happy days. After starting off with gratitude and thinking of ways to fill my day, I work out for an hour, maybe two if I have a trainer. I eat a simple breakfast—either yogurt or fruit and eggs—and then I'm off to the races.

When it comes to lunch and dinner, I have six to eight items that I'll eat. **I stick with those choices because I'm eating to live, not living to eat.** Too many people waste time and energy trying to figure out their next meal. I want that decision to be as simple as possible.

University of Michigan football coach Jim Harbaugh uses a system I like. He has three choices for many things in life. His closet, for example, is organized into game day clothes, banquet clothes, and work clothes. Then he has three options for lunch and picks one without a second thought. For these menial decisions, he doesn't waste time.

SETTING YOURSELF UP FOR A HAPPY DAY

I've learned a bunch of ways to make each day a happy one. What makes you happy will be different from what makes me happy, so your days will look different from mine.

I mentioned earlier making note of new experiences that make you happy. To elaborate on that point, when you have a good day, pay attention to the factors that made it good.

- How much sleep did you get?
- What's the quality of your sleep?
- What did you eat that day? How did it make you feel?
- If you worked out, what exercises did you do?

Sleep, exercise, and diet are big factors in having a happy day. What I learned from Dr. Breus, a well-known sleep doctor, is that sleep plays a huge role in your day-to-day happiness. A lot of people don't feel they need much sleep. Dr. Breus showed me that sleep and rest are vitally important. You've got to learn the optimal amount of sleep you need to function at a high level. It's a different amount for everyone. If I get six-and-a-half hours, I'm golden, so that's what I aim to get on a daily basis. Your needs will be different.

A big shift occurred for me when I stopped falling asleep

and began preparing for sleep. I looked at what I was doing in the two hours before I went to bed. Usually it was staring at my phone, answering work emails in bed moments before I laid my head down. Now I try to wind down by watching a meaningless TV show or game, or listening to music. I also try to get to sleep around the same time every night. The decisions I make well before my head hits the pillow have a big impact on the quality of my sleep.

Even if you're working on a big project and you're facing a late night with little sleep, you can still rest. Lounging on the couch or lying in bed lets your body and mind recover.

Eating the right foods also sets me up to have happy days. I used to chow down on foods that are hard to digest, like steak, bagels, and pizza. Those days had to end because I spent the rest of the day feeling like crap when I ate those foods. I found foods that gave me energy and added them to my go-to foods list and my go-to snacks list because I know now that fueling your body is fundamental to creating purposeful energy.

I'm not saying you should deprive yourself of foods that don't give you good energy. I won't let my focus on proper nutrition keep me from black-and-white cookies. They make me happy! But if I indulge, I'll try to adjust my meals or get in an extra workout.

HOW DO YOU GET TO YOUR RIGHT LEVEL OF ENERGY EACH DAY?

"On the deepest level, we are all energy."

—UNKNOWN

I study my happy days to see what kind of energy I'm going to need for them. If I have a lot of meetings one day, I'll eat light. If I'm playing basketball, shopping with the family, or going to a game, I'll eat foods with a lot of protein or snack on energy bars. Everyone's energy needs vary based on what their happy days look like.

As I've gotten older, pace has become a bigger issue in managing my energy. I won't deny that I want to tackle the world all in one day, but I've got to make sure I have enough gas in the proverbial fuel tank to reach that destination by day's end. I use my MVP list to pace myself and make sure I'm taking care of what's most important.

"Today you have never been this old before and will never be this young again. Right now matters!"

—DAN CLARK

Planning out your meals to suit your energy needs gives you a huge advantage, yet few people do it. Domino's Pizza once conducted a study to see what percentage of people knew what they were having for dinner at 4:30 p.m. The results were insane: 78 percent of people hadn't decided what to eat for dinner by that time. It was a big win for Domino's, who advertised more in the later afternoon, hoping to snag hungry people who wanted something convenient, like a pizza for dinner. I'm guessing if Domino's had looked at the lunch-time window, the percentage of clueless eaters would've been even higher. I decided I wasn't going to be one of those clueless people, so I started putting a lot of thought and energy into planning my meals for the day so I'd end up in a healthy place.

You know where you're going to sleep at night and where you're going to work. With that said, our meals deserve the same level of careful attention and planning. I know where I work and where I live, so I make sure I have healthy food and snacks at both places. That way, it's easier to make consistent healthy choices and have consistent healthy habits.

If you need help finding foods that'll give you energy, I recommend the book *Fit for Life*. After reading the book for the first time, I called up one of the authors, Harvey Diamond, and picked his brain about what makes up a healthy diet. I modeled a lot of my diet off what I read and what we discussed—plenty of fruit throughout the day, lean proteins like chicken, turkey, and fish, plus some salads for lunch or dinner.

When you're looking to increase your purposeful energy

by getting healthy, I learned from experience that you shouldn't start with exercise, but by looking at your diet.

This was an aha moment for me. For years, I'd spun my wheels with fitness because I was putting exercise first and not giving my diet much attention. I was trying and failing to outwork bad nutrition. Once I put my diet first, my fitness improved substantially.

I'm not here to tell you what to eat or not eat. There are some obvious broad strokes, like not making pizza, cookies, muffins, and sodas staples of your diet, but within the basic guardrails exists enough nuance that blanket advice is not helpful. Pick up some books on proper nutrition that can create a lifestyle change, not a dieting book. If you can afford it, a nutritionist can help you select foods that work for your life.

With proper rest and a healthy diet, exercise will be more beneficial.

In my late forties, I learned that in addition to changing my habits, I also needed to change my expectations. My body at almost fifty years old didn't work the same as my twenty-year-old body. When I was young, I could easily work out and lose five or ten pounds in a week. That wasn't going to happen as I moved into my fifties. That ship had sailed. I had to work much harder and much longer to lose two or three pounds.

I know we've covered this already, but it's worth repeating here because unrealistic expectations can derail someone's progress when they make changes.

Don't make getting healthy all about your weight. **Focus more on gaining health, not just losing weight.** Purposeful energy comes from a healthy body, not just a number on the scale.

Healthy changes alter your body composition, meaning the amount of muscle, body fat, protein, and water in your body will change. It's important to know your body composition because you can't manage what you can't measure. The result you're seeking is low body fat and high muscle composition. When you add muscle, you might weigh more than you would if you just focused on losing weight. People can be skinny but still be unhealthy if they have a high percentage of body fat and a low percentage of muscle mass.

I never liked lifting weights. I can't believe how much of a wimp I am, but I never lifted a weight until I was forty. But I realized that adding muscle is important as you age because you'll start to lose muscle mass in your forties. My trainer told me I was leaning, and at the same time, I went to the doctor and learned I was half an inch shorter. It was flipping me out! I had to make changes so I wouldn't wind up brittle in my fifties and sixties. I didn't want to be the old person who leaned when they walked or who got seriously injured by falling because I lacked balance and was leaned over everywhere I went.

PURPOSEFUL ENERGY IS WORTH THE EFFORT

"Health isn't owned. It's leased, and the rent is due every day."
—UNKNOWN

In my thirties, my purpose was selfish and materialistic. I was going for the money grab and sacrificing my health in pursuit of it. I can't tell you how many nights I didn't sleep or how many times I had pizza or a burger and fries for "dinner" at 10:00 p.m. prior to selling my company. Unbeknownst to me at the time, I was going down a slippery slope.

Now I know the only path to extraordinary achievement comes with purpose, and to chase that purpose, you need energy. I wish I'd known this in my twenties! I'm playing catch up from years of bad habits, but if you're reading this and you're under the age of forty, you've got the advantage of knowing what's coming, which means you can plan for it.

Even in your twenties, it's time to look ahead, to play the long game. If you want to be highly effective throughout your life, your nutrition and fitness decisions will have a direct impact. If you operate at the highest level of energy and clarity, which you get from sleep, exercise, and food, you're going to perform better and have happier days.

If you haven't played the long game (I didn't) and you reach your forties and your body starts to break down (like it did for me), it will take a lot longer to recover. Even the smallest changes before reaching that age make a difference. Trust me, you want to create some padding for yourself. It's easier to pick up a few new habits than undo decades of bad habits all at once. That revolutionary process is not fun. It's easier and more efficient to evolve. Start planning for the health you want now and make small changes along the way.

Finally, you're not going to get healthy unless you have a *why*. I want to be able to do things with my grandchildren. As a younger man, my *why* was playing basketball with my son as an adult. Now I want to be able to keep playing with him and play pickup games in the park with kids who are younger than me. You need your *why*, your purpose, whether it's fitting into your clothes, or waking up feeling better, or even having more sex with your spouse.

Once you have your motivation for fitness, it's time to

execute on that purpose. Remember Joe Plumeri's saying, "Execution eats strategy for lunch."

CHAPTER 8

LIFESTYLE GAME PLAN

"It's not what happens to you. It's what you do with what happens."

Soon after selling my company, I had a serious wake-up call. Looking back, I'm so thankful I did. I remember the day well...it was the day I found out I was obese.

Truth is, I woke up most days not feeling well. I wasn't sleeping through the night. I was going through the motions of being healthy, but it was a half-assed effort.

I decided one morning that I'd had enough of feeling tired, achy, and shitty, so I visited Dr. Bloom, a health guru who'd been recommended to me. The first thing he said to me was that I needed to focus on gaining health, not losing weight. I then underwent a body composition scan to see what percentage of my body was water, fat, muscle, and protein.

With the results in hand, Dr. Bloom told me in a soft, but firm, voice, "Brandon, you're at 26 percent body fat. This means you are obese."

I was stunned. Dr. Bloom practically had to pick my jaw up off the floor.

"Because of the type of person you are and the job you have, your stress levels are through the roof," he continued. "This is causing your weight and body fat level to be high."

That was the day I learned that stress can be fattening and that I wasn't in touch with my body at all. I was sprinting enthusiastically in the wrong direction, drinking all sorts of juices and Gatorade because I thought it was healthy. I had no idea how much harm I was doing to my nutrition with my decisions. Dr. Bloom helped me see that I needed to change what I ate and how often I ate, opting for several smaller meals throughout the day.

I had another problem, though. At forty-one years old, I was dealing with arthritis and taking some serious medication ("serious" is probably an understatement) to deal with it. Not only was the medicine not helping my condition, but it was making me feel crazy.

I decided to visit a doctor my wife's cousin swore by, Dr. Horrowitz, to get a second opinion for my arthritis. After examining me, Dr. Horrowitz said he would write me a prescription. He scribbled a few words on his prescription pad and handed the slip to me.

It said, "Lose weight. Eat better. Exercise more."

"Brandon, the medicines you're on are for people in wheelchairs who can't walk," Dr. Horrowitz explained. "For your arthritis, the best thing you can do is get healthier."

These two doctor visits gave me the push I needed to begin pursuing my health the same way I'd pursued wealth for so many years. Whatever I'd done to my body, it wasn't too late to undo the damage. It would be a tough journey, but as I've come to understand, our body is our biggest asset. LeBron James spends $1.5 million each year maintaining his body.

What kind of investment was I willing to invest in my most important asset?

I started reaching out to experts who could help me

understand the pillars of a healthy, happy, and success-ful life. My blog has over half a million readers today, but honestly, it started out for selfish reasons. I wanted to learn the best ways to gain health, improve as a parent, and receive spiritual guidance from the best people who knew the most.

The funny part about writing a blog that gets sent to your friends and family is that not only am I helping educate them (along with myself), but they hold me accountable. If they see me eating a burger and fries after I wrote about the dangers of a high-fat diet, they're not going to let me off the hook for my food choices no matter what excuses I give them!

When it comes to health, I've discovered it's not about the game. It's about the game plan. I know now what it takes to live a healthy life, but where I was falling short earlier in my life was not planning for the health I wanted. When my health started to decline, I looked for patches that inevitably fell by the wayside in favor of seemingly bigger priorities. At that point, I was waking every morning in pain because I hadn't made any changes.

Now I understand there are no discounts, coupons, or shortcuts to good health. A lifestyle game plan is the only path to success, and I've got to take the stairs to get there.

IMPROVING MY MINDSET

We're going to start with the most important component of a lifestyle game plan: not diet, not exercise, but your mindset. You don't need luck, physical strength, or God-given ability to have a winning game plan for your life. You do, however, need the right mental makeup. You need a strategy but also confidence in your own ability. Show me somebody who is executing a game plan effectively, and I'll show you somebody who is self-confident and believes in the strategy they've set forth.

But when you don't have confidence in your game plan or your ability to execute it, you'll start to feel the pressure. Have you ever seen someone who's trying to cut an insane amount of weight, like ten pounds in two weeks? They always look stressed because they know, deep down, that they don't have a winning game plan.

A game plan to gain health shouldn't lead you to stressful moments.

I realized that although I wanted to lose weight and gain health, I didn't have a big bucket of *whys*. As I pursued better health, here were some of the purposes driving me forward:

- I'd bought a new wardrobe to motivate me to lose weight, but those outfits had been sitting in my closet for several years. I was determined to fit into those clothes. (It's very embarrassing when your wife asks you, "What's up with those clothes?")

- I was booking more speaking engagements, but when I went back and watched the tape from the events, I wasn't happy with the way I looked on stage.
- I wanted to play basketball with Crosby, Keith, their friends, as well as my friends, but I didn't have the stamina for it. There's nothing like schooling a nineteen-year-old when they think you're too old to play.

It's great that I wanted to be physically fit, make money, or have a strong spiritual connection, but why do you want those things? I would need purposeful energy to make them happen, and unless those dreams had the deep roots of purpose attached, the busyness of the world would pull me away from my game plan. If that were to happen, I knew I wouldn't make the changes necessary to create the energy I needed.

I started to enjoy a little success on my journey to gain health, but failure came when I lost focus on why I was doing what I was doing and started making excuses. It was a tough lesson for me to learn, but I saw I needed to stay away from the excuse game and own up. Instead of looking for shortcuts, discounts, or coupons, I needed to dig in.

My lifestyle game plan was not a diet or exercise plan, because I knew that a short-term game plan like that wouldn't hold up long term. After talking to several experts, I came to realize there is no straight line to good health, only twists and turns. Everyone is different in their needs when it comes to what to eat and not to eat. I had to remember that it's not survival of the fittest when it comes to learning about great health. It's survival of the most flexible. With my lifestyle game plan, I was able to handle life's curveballs because I was rooted in purpose.

Back before selling the company, my calendar was chaotic and my life was twisted with busyness. I was trying to keep my head above water from one day to the next, so it felt as if life was happening to me, like I was a passenger in my own life. Now, my lifestyle game plan keeps me engaged with my life. I have a plan, which means I'm in the driver's seat.

I didn't want to wake up one day and realize my career was ending and I had no idea how to fill the next two or three decades. I didn't want to get sick and be in such bad shape that my body couldn't fight the illness. With a game plan that's rooted in purpose, now I know I can create the purposeful energy needed to handle any situation life throws at me.

Not only that, now I'm able to see issues when they pop

up because I'm focused on the right priorities. I'm not barreling forward and blocking out "distractions" in the pursuit of making more money. My eyes are on the real prizes.

If I were to share anything with you from what I've learned, it's that it's difficult to accomplish anything on an extraordinary level without a purpose. People often get caught up in goal-setting, such as losing twenty pounds. But diet and exercise plans don't last because they're propped up by goals and not fueled by purpose. It helped me to start with a defined purpose, like being able to play basketball with my son.

One of my purposes in desiring to make a lot of money is to provide for my wife and kids. A lack of money was a big factor in my life growing up, so I want it to be a nonfactor in my family life now. I work hard to earn money to avoid that stress and that conflict.

EVALUATE YOUR PURPOSE

Over the years, I've come to realize the importance of evaluating my purposes. I need to check and see if the purposes I created a decade ago still light my fire like they once did. Sometimes I'll find a purpose that still has deep roots, but those roots need to reach out a little further. This happened when I had children. When Mara and I got married, my purpose was serving her and helping provide a living for us both. The birth of my children added people to my world that I wanted to serve with all my heart, mind, and energy.

Don't be afraid to have multiple purposes. When you hit those bumps in the road, you can reach into that bucket and pull out a different *why* to keep you going. Life can get messy. When you can pull out your *whys* and remember the reasons you married your spouse, why you became friends with that person, or why you went to work for that company, you'll be inspired to push through the tough times instead of giving up.

I'm often amazed when a couple has been married fifty years. I have to ask myself, *Don't you think they've had to reset their purpose several times?* Of course. Then I'll ask, *Don't you think having a bucket of whys was instrumental in keeping their marriage going?* No doubt. Successful marriages don't just happen. They require attention and intention.

One of the first things I did during my reset was to go back and think of all the reasons why I got married in the first place. Those *whys* had been there all along. I simply wanted to revisit them to make sure I wasn't taking any positive aspect of my marriage for granted.

For a lifestyle game plan, you don't just need purpose—

you need the right purpose and many of them. Truth be told, you can't have enough *whys*.

For years, I operated without a lifestyle game plan. At some points, things got scary. When I boarded the wild ride moving out of my twenties into my thirties, my life was off-kilter and lacking clarity. I thought I was on the right track at the time, but looking back, there were some things that were mixed up. Truthfully, I could have used a better perspective. Those years with the wrong purpose and a lacking game plan took a toll on my friendships, relationships, and physical well-being. I'm proud of what I did in building my business and growing parts of the sports industry, but I'm sad about things I missed that could've been part of my life had I lived with a purpose and a game plan. I try to live my life now as if life is rigged in my favor.

If you're like I was, you have to realize that life is an inside job. (I love that phrase from Ken Blanchard.) What happens outside of work has an effect on what happens inside of work. You have to be able to step outside of yourself and realize that bad habits may be limiting your effectiveness. I never took the time to do that, and it cost me. Keep in mind that your activity level doesn't equate with your achievement level. Simply doing a lot doesn't mean you're accomplishing a lot. Extraordinary achievement requires energy, focus, diligence, and clarity.

You need to be effective and efficient. (Note to the young ones: remember, there is no app or shortcut to find these traits!) To do that, you need to have time to think, rest, eat right, enjoy your family and friends, and exercise often.

It's all about being well rounded. You hear a lot about living a balanced life, but that's BS. Nobody's life is perfectly balanced, and if it is, they're probably bored to death. What's important is realizing when you're letting one area of your life dominate the other areas and you've lost respect for all the pillars that will lead you to success. My friend Harvey Mackay helped me see that you have to be careful not to get too one-dimensional. I was so deep into building my business that I couldn't hold a conversation if it wasn't about sports or Steiner Sports. Honestly, it was pathetic, and I was on a mission to change that quickly.

You may get away with living like hell for a while, but it won't work in the long game. Think about it. The objective isn't to get married; it's to stay married and find joy with the same person for fifty plus years. Professionally, the objective isn't to earn money. It's to build a career that provides for your family and adds value to your business and your customers for a long time. **I like to say that consistency over time equals credibility.**

Having the right priorities opens the door for more happy

days. I realized one of the reasons I didn't have enough happy days was because I didn't plan enough happy days. I also hadn't taken the time to stop and notice what a happy day looked like. I just knew I was unhappy, which led to me making excuses and blaming other people.

Eventually I realized that I was the one to blame for my lacking happiness, so I started moving ahead by owning up and taking responsibility. I made evolutionary changes, not revolutionary changes, because I knew that change wouldn't happen overnight.

DON'T CHASE SUCCESS, CHASE THE THINGS THAT MAKE YOU SUCCESSFUL

One final thing I learned about the purpose attached to my lifestyle game plan that is vitally important is that it can't be about making money. I'm not saying it's bad to make money. I would encourage you to make as much money as you can. I'm saying money isn't what gets me out of bed in the morning. Money is one of the by-products of the value I add to the world. It's merely a result of my commitment to a purpose, not the result in and of itself.

Speaking from experience, chasing money could lead to unhealthy behavior and will sometimes sabotage your well-being in other areas of life. It's one thing when you're on a run for a year or two to build your business. Things go off the rails when you're on a run for twenty years and the only thing in your life is that one thing. Your business is booming, but your health is failing, you're a stranger to your family, and you're spiritually bankrupt.

It's totally fine to be career-oriented. I was for a long time, but I learned the hard way how important it is to play the long game and pace yourself. I had to make sure my reach didn't extend my grasp. I came to see that no purpose, no matter how noble, was worth burning out. **I stopped chasing success and started chasing the things that made me successful.**

A career orientation can devolve into a money fascination. In the US, we overemphasize celebrity, fame, money, job title, clout, our address, and the clothes we wear. I learned that these trappings are fool's gold that provide a false sense of happiness, and the things we have are just things. We view those blessed with fortune and fame as the lucky ones. What we don't see is how many of the rich and famous struggle with depression or paranoia. Their vast wealth disguises a life that is often hollow. Many times, it's all flash and no substance.

I mentioned that a lifestyle game plan requires being well rounded. Money is the biggest stumbling block I see to achieving this, so it's easy to pick on. Truthfully, any area of your life can cause you to stumble in this regard, even the virtuous pursuits. You can't spend every day in the gym and never see your family. By the same token, you can't do everything for your family and never darken the doorstep of a gym or a church.

I realized leaning too much in one direction was blinding me to the signs life was giving me in other areas, signs that were critical to the success of my lifestyle game plan. Playing the long game and being well rounded gave me a better perspective to see signs that my life was off track, signs telling me when I needed to focus on my health, signs that my family needed my attention. Signs come in all shapes and sizes. Some are like a flashing neon sign they're so obvious. Think about my doctor friend, John, and his heart stent. Some signs are not as obvious, and if I don't pay attention, I'll miss them.

Some signs tell me I'm on the right path. When I have a happy day now, I make note. When the people around me are happy, I keep doing what I'm doing. In the past, I was too quick to point out what disappointed me and too slow to seek out what brought me joy.

"Life moves pretty fast. If you don't stop and look around once in a while, you could miss it."

—FERRIS BUELLER FROM *FERRIS BUELLER'S DAY OFF*

I'm reminded of the time I was with my family at a restaurant in China. The meal was so good we wanted to order some more, but we couldn't decide which things to order. I told the waiter to just bring out the whole meal again. The waiter thought we were crazy, but the meal was too amazing to walk away from, and I didn't know if we'd ever be back.

If something is going great, I keep hitting that button, just like with the old arcade games when I'd get a high score and was rewarded with an extra game. If I have a great day with my family, I replay that day. I don't want to ignore those positive signs in my life.

EATING TO LIVE, NOT LIVING TO EAT

If you had seen me fifteen years ago, you would not think I'd be in a position to talk about nutrition, let alone write about it in a book. I'm not going to share a picture, but let's just say I was more apt to be making funeral arrangements than arrangements to write another book. Since then, I've learned some things from top nutrition experts, and I thought it would be helpful to share some of the insights I've discovered about my body, the foods I need to eat for good energy, and the foods I used to eat that no longer make me feel good.

Eating right is a big point with me around our office. I'll

often ask my employees, "What you're eating might work for you right now, but will it work in ten years?" Some of them don't understand that fast food in their twenties is doable, but it'll be hard to wean off that diet as they approach thirty. Furthermore, I don't think they want to wait a decade before they see how double cheeseburgers and fries affect their heart and their waistline.

My mindset shift in recent years has been that I eat to live, I don't live to eat. I totally understand how tough this change is for most people. Part of the difficulty comes from the fact that our gratification culture has warped our dietary choices. You're not unique when you say you love to eat. Everyone loves eating! Nobody wakes up dreading the fact they've got to consume food throughout the day to survive.

A lot of us grow up seeing poor dietary habits modeled at home, so we don't know any better until we're adults and a lot of damage has already been done. I couldn't have had worse training the first twenty years of my life. When I was a kid, we ate fast food for almost every meal. We regularly ate pizza and hot dogs. Things only got worse when I got to college and added alcohol and chicken wings to the mix.

What made the difference was understanding how I made food choices. Was I deciding with my brain or with my emotions? I never realized how my decision-making was affected by having kids, running a business, and dealing with the day-to-day stresses of life. Sure, the occasional emotional choice was fine, but my emotions were the prevailing decision-maker in my diet far too often, which meant I was making a lot of bad food choices.

I had to stop giving my emotions a vote in what I ate. The Little Brandon inside me who wanted black-and-white cookies every day had his voting privileges revoked on what to eat. Instead, I gave those privileges to the Little Brandon who wanted to be healthy, play basketball with his kids, and fit into his clothes. That Brandon got to decide what I ate.

As I got older, it became more important for me to eat what was good for me, not necessarily what I liked or what was easy. Once I made those changes, though, what I found was that nutritious, energy-rich foods became my favorite foods to eat. Now it's the greasy, deep fried stuff that makes my stomach hurt. I still splurge from time to time with pizza or ice cream, but I do it far less often than I did when I was younger.

I have to remind myself before I eat that the only reason food exists is to fuel my body and give me energy for the things I need to do, not give me thirty seconds of satisfaction. Food wasn't put on this planet to be the most joyous activity I do all day. To help with this struggle, I pull out my *whys* and remind myself of the reasons I want to be healthy.

PAY ATTENTION TO WHAT YOU EAT

I try to analyze how I feel after eating certain foods. If I wake up not feeling well, I look back to what I ate and try to avoid those foods. What you eat and how you feel are directly correlated. I see it when my employees are unproductive on a Monday because they spent their weekend partying, eating chicken wings, and drinking a bunch of beer. Here's the thing: if you blow off forty or fifty Mondays per year, and you've been in the workplace for twenty years, how much productivity have you lost because your food choices over the weekend made your life miserable come Monday morning?

When combined with a lack of exercise, a poor diet also leads to serious health problems. According to *Living Without Pain* author Harvey Diamond, ninety million Americans wake up every day in pain. Ailments like arthritis and diabetes are influenced by age and genetics, but they can be avoided with proper diet and exercise.

Over the years, I have to wonder how much more productive I could have been, how much more money I could have made, if I had paid more attention to how I treated my body. I'd like to tell my younger self, "Get in touch with your body and take notice of the signs it's giving you, like pain or weakness. You'll be grateful you did the older you get."

By paying attention to my body and my energy needs, I learned I have hypoglycemia, which means I have to eat often to keep my blood sugar levels up. I eat four meals a day and snack often. Snacking often is dangerous because we tend to take it too far, so it's important that I plan to have healthy snacks both at home and at the office. I tend to snack on fruit (my top choice) with some nuts and the occasional health bar mixed in. I also enjoy snacking on raw vegetables, like carrots and celery, with some hummus.

One of the things that changed my mind on how I ate was when Dr. Bloom said to me, "Brandon, if your body was a business, it would be bankrupt." Dr. Bloom was great about relating my health to business so I could better understand what he was telling me.

It helped me understand why I needed to track my calories. If I wanted to lose weight, that's the only way it was going to happen. I wouldn't set a budget for my company and then fail to track our spending. In the same way, I needed to keep track of my calorie budget each day to make sure I wasn't overspending. Losing weight would only happen if I burned more calories than I consumed, so I started tracking every calorie (i.e., dollar).

That's why you've heard it said that you can't outwork a bad diet. If your exercise burns 1,000 calories, but you're 1,500 calories above your basic daily energy needs, you're going to gain weight. Each human being has unique dietary needs, but this basic formula applies to everyone regardless of their background, body makeup, or activity level.

Be wary of fad diets because they don't work for everyone. I jumped on the high-protein fad diet because it gave me energy and it seemed like I lost weight. Little did I know, the excessive protein was a major contributor to my kidney stones. When I went to the doctor, he told me my protein levels were more than double what a normal person should consume. That diet resulted in a couple of nice visits to the hospital.

If you struggle with hunger, make sure you're getting enough sleep. I always struggle with hunger when I'm tired, so I had to make sure I was getting enough sleep and tried to avoid getting tired. Self-control is correlated with an area in the frontal lobe of our brain called the dorsolateral prefrontal cortex. When you're sleep deprived, that part of your brain doesn't function as well, and your discipline starts to break down. In the brain of a tired, hungry person, it's OK to get some ice cream because it'll make them feel better.

Do you ever see someone at the end of a long day, when they're tired and hungry, grab the vegetables? No, that's when they grab the chips and cookies because they're starving and have zero discipline.

LISTEN TO THE SIGNS YOUR BODY GIVES YOU

Just like a not-to-do list, I have a not-to-eat list that I live by. I love bagels and muffins and have eaten them my whole life, but now I sprint away from them. They're calorie dense and are hard to digest, as they are a complex carb. They give you a little energy but nothing long-lasting, which makes me ask the Little Brandon who gets the vote on eating. "Why would you want me to put that into my body?" It's like putting water in your car instead of gas. It makes no sense. Some people start their day with a scone, which is over 600 calories. I love scones, but it's like eating ice cream. You're using about 25 percent of your daily calorie intake on one food. Why trade a fourth of my daily calories for three seconds of enjoyment?

As I got older, my taste buds changed along with how my body reacted to certain foods. By being willing to broaden my horizons, healthy foods that were once on my not-to-eat list migrated to my what-to-eat list. As a kid, I thought I'd never eat fish. Now I eat fish four or five times a week. I never thought I'd eat a salad without salad dressing. Now I know that the salad dressing has more calories than the salad.

I have a beverage once in a while, but I drink water most of the time. I used to dread drinking water. I wanted a Gatorade or Dr Pepper instead. *No mas.* What changed my mind was how I felt after drinking a soda compared to drinking lots of water.

We can all stand to drink more water. Staying hydrated is essential to feeling your best. A lot of times when you feel hungry, you're actually just dehydrated. Try drinking a glass of water instead of snacking to see if your hunger dissipates. A good rule of thumb is to drink around half your body weight in ounces of water every day. (Coffee doesn't count!)

Do you feel like crap after a long flight? What's commonly known as jet lag is actually caused by dehydration due to the cabin pressure in the airplane. Here's a tip that's been a game changer for me, given how much I fly. For every hour of your flight, drink a bottle of water. Also, plan to bring healthy snacks if you're on a flight that serves a meal. Whatever you do, don't eat the food on airplanes. These prepackaged meals are loaded with sodium, so they'll stay "good" for longer. Sodium (salt) will dehydrate you even more.

WITH EXERCISE, IT'S OK TO START SLOW

Once I had my diet in order, it was time to start thinking about exercise. I'm not a fitness expert, but I consulted with experts, including the former Yankees strength coach, Dana Cavalea, and Dori Pearson to work myself out of the terrible condition I found myself in. I wanted to have smart people advising and guiding me while I made evolutionary changes.

Two things intimidated me when it came to exercise: getting started and then getting restarted if I got sidetracked. I thought I had to dive into the deep end of the pool, but that's not the case. Starting out, exercise can be nothing more than a good, brisk walk. I got off track a few times, but when I did, I pulled out my bag of *whys* and found my focus again.

I never saw myself as someone who would lift weights, but as I got older and started to lose muscle mass, it became imperative that I add some kind of resistance training to my workout routine. The last thing I wanted was to be frail at fifty years old. Cardio was good for burning calories and slimming down, but it didn't add muscle.

I had to lift some kind of weight to retain my muscle level or eventually start to improve it.

Training with your body weight has become popular recently with old school exercises like pull-ups, push-ups, sit-ups, and planks making up the bulk of a workout.

When I was young, I never thought I could afford a trainer, but what I realized is that a trainer doesn't have to be a permanent expense. I meet with one occasionally to get new exercises, and then I do them on my own. I also use the internet to research new exercises. There are all sorts of video-based programs out there, from high-intensity-interval training to yoga, that you can watch and follow along with from the comfort of your living room.

Speaking of yoga, don't forget to stretch before and after you work out. You want to warm up and cool down your muscles when you exercise so you don't get injured.

NO ONE PLANS TO FAIL, BUT THEY FAIL TO PLAN

In trying to bring nutrition and exercise together, the key is in the planning. No one ever plans to fail, but they fail to plan. **It's not the game; it's the game plan.** Strategy is critical, but execution is more important, and the execution is tied into your bucket of *whys*.

Considering my schedule was vital to me in this endeavor. I knew I was overextended, meaning I would shove my health concerns to the side before I would drop other things. My priorities were all wrong, and I wasn't scheduling the most important areas of my life—the one-hour conversation with my wife to see what we had going on, or the exercise I needed to regain my health. I saw that if I didn't schedule those things, they wouldn't happen.

Starting with my diet, I needed to plan my meals ahead of time so I wasn't grabbing a slice of pizza in-between meetings. I had to stop leaving candy sitting around my office and at home. When I was hungry, that would be what I reached for instead of apples or almonds.

With exercise, it helped me to find the best time in my day to work out and stick to it. I like to work out thirty minutes after I wake up because nothing can interfere at that point in my day. If I'm beat after a long day at the office, the chances are slim I'm going to come home and work out. But I'm always fresh and available in the mornings.

A friend of mine recently told me he didn't think he had time to work out in the mornings. I immediately replied, "That's bullshit." I guaranteed him that if he made time a few days a week, he'd be able to get more done every day and get it done faster. I've found that if I don't work out, I'm sluggish, inefficient, and ineffective the rest of the day. My friend may have thought he didn't have time to work out, but his perspective was wrong. I believe that if something is important to you, you'll find ways to make time for it.

At the beginning of this chapter, I told you about the doctor visits that kickstarted my desire to regain my health. What I didn't share was the moment that pushed me to finally visit the doctor instead of slogging through each day feeling miserable.

We had a clinic we were doing with a company at Giants Stadium, so I brought Crosby along, and we were playing catch on the field when Carl Banks, the former linebacker for the Giants, approached me with a concerned look on his face.

He said, "Brandon, you better take it easy. I've known you a long time, and I've never seen you so heavy. I'm afraid you might have a heart attack out here."

To have such a big-name athlete be so honest with me really shattered me. It finally hit me that my health had been spiraling out of control for a long time. Rather than run from this truth, I realized that my fitness and health were a choice. I could work to get myself back on track or drop dead at sixty from a heart attack.

You never know where you'll be when life hands you a sign. When it does, will you ignore it or heed what life is trying to tell you? That moment at Giants Stadium was the spark that ignited a health revolution in my life. It wasn't easy to undo all the bad habits I'd picked up over the decades, but no other change I've made in my entire life has been that worthwhile.

CONCLUSION

At the beginning of this book, you saw me coming off one of my highest yet lowest moments. I was richer than I ever imagined I could be, but I was unhappy, unhealthy, and unfulfilled. What I've shared with you throughout this book are the lessons I learned as I went about resetting my life in the areas of faith, fortune, and fitness. Let's review some now as we close out the book.

If you lack the motivation or inspiration to do something, or you're stuck in a rut and frustrated about it, then you need to find a purpose in your life. Do you have a winnable game? Start by defining what winning looks like to you and what winning looks like to the most important people around you—spouse, children, employees, coworkers.

Keep in mind that winning isn't necessarily just about you.

For many people, their life purpose is found in helping others to win. It brings them tremendous joy. Former Yankees manager and Hall of Famer Joe Torre once told me sacrifice is more than just a bunt. You must be interested in helping others, not just yourself, win. Real success starts when selfishness ends.

Focus on your purpose. Many people seek passion, but purpose initiates passion when that purpose is sought with commitment. Seek your purpose, get committed, and passion will follow. Remember our tree metaphor: everything grows up from the roots of purpose.

Many people struggle when they graduate college because they don't have a purpose. Their purpose was to graduate, but they haven't been able to reset their purpose since getting that degree. For older people who have been doing the same thing for a long time and have accomplished goals, resetting a purpose will look different but is just as necessary.

When you have a purpose, you are like a freight train. Nothing is going to stop you unless you give it that power. Some people are stopped by a story they tell themselves that just isn't true. You have to check your story to make sure it's true. If it's not true, you've got to change your story, and if it is true, you've got to accept it before you can move on. My story is proof that it's not too late to add another chapter or correct the last chapter.

Moving on can be difficult if your story includes failure that's led to disappointment and fear. These feelings are like kryptonite to your purpose. The best way to deal with disappointment is to trade your expectations for appreciation and have faith that these setbacks are to make you better and help you grow. In the long run, you'll be better for it. You can't live in fear and faith at the same time. It's impossible. A great way to build your faith is to help others with no expectation of anything in return.

Learn to forgive and start forgiving people who have hurt you or disappointed you today. Settle those scores any way you can, and if need be, insert mercy. Forgive people even if they're not deserving because it helps to clean up those negative messes.

Purpose is an evolving process, which means you'll constantly be reinventing and resetting your *whys*. It doesn't matter how young or old you are. It's time to evaluate your purpose when you've achieved your big dreams and have nothing left to accomplish. You've gone to the highest level you can with that dream, and now it's time to reset your purpose with a newer, bigger dream to achieve.

You'll carry some purposes your entire life, such as being

healthy. You'll never achieve perfect health and be able to check that box. As long as you're alive, your health will require your constant attention. The dreams attached to that purpose might change as you get married, have kids, and ease into middle age, but the roots will remain intact.

DON'T WAIT FOR TOMORROW

Faith, fortune, and fitness are the pillars of an extraordinary life, which means they're too important to put off until tomorrow. If your schedule is filled with clutter, work to clean it up and ask for help when you need it. Stop trying to pull that 9,999-pound truck across the bridge with a 10,000-pound capacity. Days filled up with activities usually don't leave you feeling fulfilled. They're far more likely to leave you feeling burned out.

Make yourself an MVP list and a not-to-do list. When you do the most important things for the most important people, you'll have far more happy days. A lifestyle game plan also makes for happier days. When you're well rested, eating right, and exercising often, you can devote your purposeful energy to those most valuable priorities.

Don't wish that you had someone else's life. Savor the life you've been given and make the most of it. Remember that the grass isn't greener on the other

side; it's greener where you water it. If it is greener over there, I'm sure the water bill is a lot higher.

If you're struggling right now, just beat yesterday. If you follow that simple rule every day, you'll dig yourself out of whatever hole you're in quicker than you realize.

There are millions of people in our country right now who are dealing with depression, addiction, anxiety, and other mental health struggles. More and more people are taking prescription drugs to help them cope with these conditions. My hope is that what you've read in this book can help you if you're struggling with these or other problems. I know living with purpose helped pull me out of the haze I was in after I sold my company. It wasn't easy, but the changes I've made in the past sixteen years have saved my life.

WHAT IF YOU COULD TALK TO GOD?

I know I've shared a lot of the lessons I learned so far in this book, but I've got to share a few more from one of my all-time favorite moves. *Oh God!* is a 1977 film directed by Carl Reiner starring John Denver and George Burns. John Denver plays Jerry Landers, an assistant manager at a supermarket. At the supermarket one day, an elderly man who claims to be God (Burns) approaches Jerry and recruits him to be his messenger.

I don't want to spoil the movie for any of you who may be interested in checking it out, but here's a memorable quote from God I have to share:

> I know how hard it is in these times to have faith. But maybe if you could have the faith to start with, maybe the times would change. You could change them. Think about it. Try. And try not to hurt each other. There's been enough of that. It really gets in the way. I'm a God of very few words and Jerry's already given you mine. However hopeless, helpless, mixed up, and scary it all gets, it can work. If you find it hard to believe in me, maybe it would help you to know that I believe in you.

That's a nice word about living in faith, isn't it? One of the things I love about that movie is how it answers so many of the toughest questions about faith with relative ease.

Here's an exchange from *Oh God!* that I think about a lot:

> Jerry: "Uh, sometimes, uh, now and then, couldn't we just talk?"

> God: "I'll tell you what. You talk, I'll listen."

Even though it's a movie, I do believe God is listening. Considering how everything today is so complicated politically, with gun violence, suicide, addiction, and more plaguing us each day, maybe we need to step back and realize that we're causing it. Maybe it's time for us to start talking to God a lot more. I've got to believe he's pretty open-minded.

OPPORTUNITIES TO CONNECT

If you enjoyed this book, I'd love the opportunity to connect with you further. My first two books, *You Gotta Have Balls* and *The Business Playbook*, can be picked up on my personal website, BrandonSteiner.com. If you go to the site, you can subscribe to my *What Else?* blog and listen to the podcast I host called *Unplugged*. I also host a live Q&A television series called *Project X* that teaches entrepreneurs how to take their idea further.

The blog includes posts about sex, health, sports, winning and losing—just a wide variety of topics with plenty of true stories included. On the podcast, I talk with athletes, coaches, successful business people, and celebrities from many different arenas.

CONNECT WITH ME ON SOCIAL MEDIA

Website: BrandonSteiner.com
Facebook: facebook.com/Steiner
Twitter and Instagram: @BrandonSteiner
LinkedIn: linkedin.com/in/brandonsteiner

I've written over 1,500 blog posts, which is funny because anyone who knows me knows I'm half-illiterate. I get asked all the time why I put out so much content. I shared earlier that my reasons for starting the blog were selfish. I wanted to connect with doctors, gurus, and all kinds of specialists who could help me get myself back in order.

But I've always loved sharing what I learn with others in the hopes it will help them. In fact, what I'm most proud of is how relatable my content is to the lives of my readers. I'm not writing 2,000-word essays. My stuff is short and easy to understand. It's meant to inspire you to action, and given the feedback from my readers, it does. I get emails daily from people who were positively affected by these resources, and that's a wonderful feeling.

What started as a blog has led to me having over one million followers on Facebook and over 650,000 blog readers. I guess you could call me an influencer now, but I'd rather help people than influence them.

This process has helped me see that when you start with doing good, it'll lead to you doing well if you have faith. In addition to the success with my blog and on social media, my desire to help people has started a second career for me speaking to different groups and leading workshops where I share my sales and leadership experience, along with lessons I've learned. With this second act in my life, I'm able to take the money I make and pour it into charities and causes Mara and I believe in. It's been a tremendous blessing.

STEINERISMS

Steinerisms are the smartest things I've heard from people I know—friends, mentors, even acquaintances. I look at life as an opportunity to learn from others and improve myself. The world is a classroom, and everybody is a teacher. I never discount what I can learn from someone. Since the age of twenty-one, when I pick up a nugget I like, I jot it down. Over time, I'll add my perspective to the idea and create my own nugget of wisdom: a Steinerism, if you will.

I've been collecting bits of wisdom and adding my own flavor to them since college. I'm sharing these Steinerisms with you here in the hopes they'll enrich your life like they have mine. Perhaps they can give you a new perspective you never considered before.

I'm also including some of my favorite quotes from incredibly smart people.

While not an exhaustive list, here are a few of my favorites:

- If you want a rainbow, you gotta deal with the rain.
- "The opposite of wealth accumulation is generosity. The opposite of recognition is service."—Ken Blanchard
- "We are either green and growing or ripe and rotting, but never standing still."—David Corbin
- If you leave your growth to randomness, you're heading for mediocrity.
- I am not only an overachiever, I am an overbeliever.
- Change is inevitable except from a vending machine.
- "Money motivates neither the best people nor the best in people. Purpose does."—Nilofer Merchant
- What are the GAPs (game altering plays) that could help change your life?
- Success is a path. Significance is a path and a journey.
- Failure is not a person. There is a difference between the person and the performance.
- Don't measure yourself by what you have accomplished but by what you should have accomplished with your ability, along with the opportunity you were given.
- Three things I want from the people I work with: 1) Dream big; 2) Get shit done; 3) Want to have fun.

- "Pursue excellence; ignore success. If you pursue excellence, success will be a by-product. If you pursue success for the sake of success, you will be disappointed."—Deepak Chopra
- Never eat ballpark food before the third inning or the end of the first quarter—it's left over from the game before.
- What would you do for a person who you knew couldn't do anything for you?
- A big part of who you are is who raised you and where you grew up.
- "Two keys to abundant living: caring about others and sharing with others."—William Arthur Ward
- Do as much as you can for as many people as you can without expecting anything in return.
- Commitment is not always convenient.
- My mother always said, "Give to give. Don't give to get."
- Relationships are a mirror. If you are unhappy with your wife, she is probably unhappy with you. Same goes for employees.
- All communication is not equal. For the youth that may be reading this, don't be afraid to write a note or pick up the phone to say hello, thank you, or to check in.
- In negotiating, a big part of getting what you want is helping other people get what they need.
- Thinking you want to be happy is not as important as understanding you deserve to be happy.

- Your true value is determined by how much you give in value, rather than how much you take in payment.
- Don't let a bump in the road put you on the side of the road, in a ditch.
- The end only justifies the means if good people don't get hurt along the way.
- Rome wasn't built in a day, but I'm sure they were working every day to build it.
- "Dig the well before you're thirsty."—Harvey Mackay
- Are you spending your time or investing your time?
- "Just because you're a character doesn't mean you have character."—The Wolf in *Pulp Fiction*
- Your best days are not your yesterdays.

ACKNOWLEDGMENTS

I want to thank my family—Mara, Nicole, Crosby, Keith, and my brother Adam—for their unconditional support throughout the years.

Thank you to my friends at the Harvey Mackay Round-table who have helped me by showing me how to grow and be a better person.

Thank you to Josh Raymer for your help putting this book together.

Thank you to Dr. Phil and Susan G. for helping keep my life on track. I also want to thank Dr. Bloom, Dr. Lerner, Dr. Zarowitz, Dr. Geller, and Dr. Spivak. Thanks to Nick Resvey, Dori Pearson, Antoine Johnson, and Dana Cavalea for keeping me in one piece.

ABOUT THE AUTHOR

BRANDON STEINER started the company that would later become known as Steiner Sports (then called Steiner Associates) in 1987. He started with $4,000, a one-room office, and an intern. After spending the first part of his career in the food service and hospitality industry, working for Hyatt Hotels, Hard Rock Cafe, and the Sporting Club, Brandon had developed relationships with enough high-profile athletes to start a company that booked corporate appearances and speaking engagements for his clients.

It was the mid-'90s when Brandon had an aha moment on a crowded train headed into work. He saw a photo of Mark Messier on the back page of every passenger's newspaper. Messier was holding the Stanley Cup after snapping the New York Rangers title drought, and as he looked at the photo, Brandon envisioned a signed photo that his company could sell to die-hard Rangers fans. It was the beginning of the next phase for Steiner Sports, one that would make them the country's leading sports collectible business.

Brandon still runs Steiner Sports, which has worked with some of the most famous athletes and teams in the world. In 2004, the company struck a deal with the New York Yankees to become the team's memorabilia provider. Steiner Sports has similar deals with Notre Dame's football team, Syracuse Athletics, and Madison Square Garden. Among its exclusive athletes are Steph Curry, Chris Paul, Eli Manning, and Derek Jeter.

In addition to running Steiner Sports, Brandon is also a media personality and sought-after speaker. He's a frequent guest on 98.7 FM/ESPN-NY Radio and serves as the cohost of the YES Network's *Yankees-Steiner: Memories of the Game* series. He's given talks at major universities, including Harvard and Yale, and at several Fortune 500 companies.

Brandon is the author of two other books—*The Business*

Playbook, published in 2003, and *You Gotta Have Balls*, published in 2012. Both are available for purchase on his personal website: BrandonSteiner.com. His popular "What Else?" blog, with more than half a million subscribers, can also be found on his website. In addition to the blog, Brandon hosts a popular podcast called *Unplugged* and a live Q&A television show broadcast on Facebook Live called *Project X*. Both feature in-depth interviews with prominent businesspeople, entrepreneurs, authors, and athletes that dive into their life's journey, their trials and tribulations, and their stories of success.

Brandon is dedicated to giving back to his community. He was instrumental in helping found the Falk College Department of Sport Management at his alma mater, Syracuse University. He supports several charities, but one of his favorites is Family Services of Westchester, a not-for-profit organization that helps provide quality social and mental health services to its clients. With Brandon's help, the organization was able to open two group homes for teenage boys and girls who have no place to call home.

Brandon lives in Scarsdale, New York, with his wife Mara, to whom he's been happily married for thirty years. They have three children: Crosby, Nicole, and Keith. He bleeds Syracuse orange and enjoys hosting pickup basketball games at his house twice a week for friends, colleagues, professional athletes, celebrities, and anyone else who will pass him the ball.

Finally—and perhaps most importantly—Brandon invented the everything bagel in 1973 when he was fourteen. He was a part-time baker at a Brooklyn bagel shop when, late one night, he threw all the toppings onto one bagel to see what would happen.

The rest, as they say, is delicious history.

20124737R00149

Made in the USA
Middletown, DE
09 December 2018